ENDORSEMENTS

Like co-sojourner Doug McMurry, my life was profoundly transformed by a series of prayer meetings with Dick Simmons in 1983 breaking the power of the Bagwhan Rajneesh cult on the soil of my home state of Oregon. Doug now brings to light stories of God's faithfulness in the first 700 years of history that were refreshingly new to me, concluding with heroes and heroines of authentic faith like Oswald, Aiden and Hilda. For the first time I understood the ramifications of the shift from "By-My-Spirit" kingdom to "Power-and-Might" religion at the Synod of Whitby. I was especially stirred by the three core components that kept the Desert Fathers and the Celts in the flow of the Spirit: houses of prayer, discipleship communities and soul friendships. As we find ourselves in a dark season of pandemic pain and geo-political peril, I agree with my fellow pioneer, Doug-- we are postured and poised for a Third Great Awakening. *"Come Holy Spirit!"*

–Tom White

Founder and President, Frontline Ministries; Global Hub Leader with Movement.org.; Author, *The Believer's Guide to Spiritual Warfare* and *The Practitioner's Guide: Building City Gospel Movements*

Through our partnership in the Gospel over the last 26 years, I have heard Doug McMurry's voice on numerous occasions. I am very familiar with it. However, never has his voice spoken more clearly and passionately than in *Glory Through Time*. From page to page you will find yourself riveted, compelled, convicted, and inspired by God's stories as told by Doug. I not only fully commend this book to you but boldly suggest that it be a must-read for all who desire to be a part of God's times of refreshing.

–Dr. Robert J. Rhoden,
President of Ascent College and Executive Director of Education for the Potomac Ministry Network of the Assemblies of God

For 30 years Doug McMurry and I have walked together, learning to cooperate with the Lord as He ignites fresh moves of the Holy Spirit. In these moves of God, Doug has provided intensive intercessory prayer and anointed teaching, to prepare us for what we believe will be the next Great Awakening—possibly the End-Times awakening when the Great Commission of the Church will be complete.

Complementing this lived experience of prayer for revival is Doug's life-long study of the advancement of the Kingdom through history. He is gifted with profound discernment of the great historic moves of God which in turn has impelled him to take part in the moves of God today—and to equip others to do so.

This combination of historical insight and practical experience are all brought together in this excellent book. This is not just a history of the great moves of God, but a series of lessons, from the stories of the past, to instruct us to have a role in this present great awakening. It is rare, if not completely unique, to have both a historian and a practitioner of revival prayer combining knowledge and experience into a single book.

As we enter this second decade of the 21st century, in which global evil is on the rise threatening the advancement of the Gospel of Jesus Christ, this book is for "such a time as this." I am convinced this book will be used by the Holy Spirit to bring God's answer to the challenges of this age, and to send the Third Great Awakening, advancing the Kingdom of God in our time.

This book will not only inspire you with stories of God's glory in the past but will equip you to take part in the future glory of His Kingdom, which is just now erupting worldwide.

–Rev. Dr. Zeb Bradford Long
Executive Director of Presbyterian
Reformed Ministries, International

The book *Glory through Time* by Doug McMurry is a wonderful read. It shows that so many values and orientations that we hold dear today are very ancient. They are always discovered by Christians of every age who seek God and an understanding through the Word with all their hearts. And God will restore and do it again.

–Daniel Juster, Th. D.
Restoration from Zion of Tikkun Global (Jerusalem)

The prophetic spirit that shone through biblical writers as a light in dark places (2 Peter 1:19), has continued to course through countless inspired people through the ages, as highlighted by Douglas McMurry: from the Perennial Praise at Comgall's Vale of Angels in Ireland to Great Awakenings in the USA. An amazing record.

—Ray Simpson

Founding Guardian of the International Community of Aidan and Hilda, www.aidanandhilda.org, (Britain)

I have known Doug McMurry for over a decade, and I highly recommend this book. His years of experience as a pastor, teacher, researcher, writer, and historian come to life in this book. Within your hands is 700 years of HIS-story (GOD's story). Doug concisely tells the story of what God has done, while provoking all to believe the best is yet to come. Each chapter richly tells the testimony of Jesus' work in the lives of ordinary people called to do extraordinary things.

—Ben Atkinson

author and director of holyclubs.com

GLORY THROUGH TIME

Vol. 1

By Douglas McMurry

A Narrative of the Kingdom of God
for the First Seven Hundred Years
Of the Christian Era

 TRILOGY

Glory Through Time, Volume 1

Trilogy Christian Publishers A Wholly Owned Subsidiary of Trinity Broadcasting Network

2442 Michelle Drive Tustin, CA 92780

Cover drawing by Douglas McMurry

Manufactured in the United States of America

10 9 8 7 6 5 4 3 2 1

Library of Congress Cataloging-in-Publication Data is available.

ISBN: 978-1-63769-386-5
E-ISBN: 978-1-63769-387-2

TABLE OF CONTENTS

FOREWORD

For thus the Lord GOD, the Holy One of Israel, has said, "In returning (repentance) and rest you will be saved, In quietness and trust is your strength." But you were not willing, And you said, "No, for we will flee on horses," Therefore you shall flee! "And we will ride on swift horses," Therefore those who pursue you shall be swift.

Isaiah 30:15-16

Why should we care about what happened in the British Isles some 1,600 years ago?

If we care about missions and expanding the Kingdom of God, what happened then is very important.

Doug McMurry's review of the first 700 years of Christianity is a masterful explication of what worked and what did not work in terms of extending the Kingdom of God starting from Jerusalem to the farthest reaches of the Roman Empire. Men and women went out at Jesus' command to proclaim the kingdom of God.

Doug contrasts two fundamental approaches to this work of preaching—perhaps it would be better to say "sharing"—the Gospel of Jesus Christ.

One method seemed to get off to a slow start taking time to pick up speed. However, it appears that once a certain critical mass was attained, it took off and whole countries and regions became Christian, not just in name but deeply and thoroughly. The Church that resulted was healthy, resilient and transformative. This method is what he refers to as "By-My-Spirit" Christianity, taken from Zechariah 4:6.

> *Then he said to me, "This is the word of the LORD to Zerubbabel saying, 'Not by might nor by power, but by My Spirit,' says the LORD of hosts."*

I like to think of this as living out Isaiah 30:15—"In returning and rest… in quietness and trust is your strength."

The contrast is reliance on "swift horses" or what he calls, "Power-and-Might" Christianity. Like in the passage above, it may move faster but it will be pursued even more rapidly by those who pursue…

Power-and-Might Christianity may seem to spread with greater speed to cover more ground and take in greater areas quickly but McMurry points out the telling fact that in less than 100 years after the whole Roman Empire was proclaimed Christian by power and by might it all came crashing down. The Christian Church that had existed in the British Isles up to that point essentially ceased to exist as Rome pulled her armies back to defend the once great city on the Tiber. This left a vacuum that was filled by indigenous tribes, tribes that had not embraced the foreign religion of the conquerors.

Into the ashes of empire, God sent those who looked not to worldly power and might but depended on the Spirit of God and God's love to extend His Kingdom. They literally refused to ride swift horses but (often literally) walked wherever they went with this Good News.

* * *

I currently live in South Korea seeking to be obedient to the work that God has given us to prepare for the opening of North Korea to the Gospel of the Kingdom. I am the fourth generation that God has sent to the Orient and to this land to proclaim His love and His salvation. I believe strongly that what Doug shows us about the supernatural power of By-My-Spirit Christianity is extremely important in this 21st Century. I know that when North Korea opens, there will be a great struggle between Power-and-Might and By-My-Spirit to bring the Gospel North. My fervent prayer is that this time of preparation will be used by God to demonstrate the true power of His Spirit and His way, that the modern Church will return and rest in God, repenting in humility. In fact, I believe that God is waiting for this to happen before He allows North Korea to be fully open, such that South Korean Christians may carry their faith to the North.

Perhaps my focus on Korea and my family's experience in Korea and China has colored my perspective but I have felt that up to now the two most important figures calling us to radical faithfulness and trust in God for the work of missions were John Nevius and Rolland Allen, both missionaries to China.

Nevius made a two-week visit to Korea in 1890 at the invitation of Horace Underwood and other pioneer Protestant missionaries. They were so convinced of the rightness of

Nevius' "three-self" approach to missions that they began immediately to apply it to their efforts in Korea. The idea of the three selves are that the Church should be self-propagating, self-supporting and self-governing.* As they applied these principles in Korea, they laid a solid foundation for the amazing expansion of the Korean Protestant Church. This approach to missions was also one of the main factors leading to the great Pyongyang Revival of 1907 that transformed the city and earned it the sobriquet of "Jerusalem of the East." (See Volume Two of *Glory Through Time* for an account of this season of Divine Presence.)

Rolland Allen's seminal work, also drawn from his experience as a missionary in China, was <u>Missionary Methods: St. Paul's or Ours</u>. (Published originally in 1912 in London by R. Scott, it was republished by Butterworth Press, Cambridge in 2006.) Allen experienced the Boxer Rebellion in China. He also travelled to India and did research in Canada and East Africa. All of this confirmed his own commitment to the Three-Self approach. A deep study of Saint Paul's methods filled out his understanding of how the Kingdom of God should be extended in total reliance upon the Holy Spirit rather than traditional methods and governmental structures—"power" missions that relied on education, organization and Western resources.

I believe that both Nevius and Allen are important for understanding how God would have us conduct the missionary enterprise, even now in the 21ˢᵗ Century. Now I add Doug

---

* Unfortunately, the Communist government of the People's Republic of China has, for ideological reasons, appropriated this term for the official government-controlled Three Self Church.

McMurry's work to that of these two giants of modern missions. *Glory Through Time* must be read and digested by anyone interested in missions or who just has a heart for the expansion of the kingdom of God.

I am excitedly awaiting Part II where he will develop his ideas through tracing this work of the Holy Spirit into the 21st Century.

Ben Torrey
Jesus Abbey's Three Seas Center
Taebaek, Korea

ACKNOWLEDGMENTS

I would like to express my appreciation to my mentor in prayer, the late Dick Simmons, who first unfolded for me and my wife the mighty deeds of God in the Great Awakenings of the past, and the unique role of Christian prayer to advance the kingdom of God. Dick not only taught the power of God in history but then, in 1983, trained a group of us in Oregon to actually try kingdom prayer—and then to see the actual power of God manifest before our eyes, delivering the state of Oregon from the curse of the Rajneeshpuram cult. My wife and I will be forever indebted to this man for discipling us in kingdom realities.

I am indebted to many others who were willing to help me shape my *Glory Through Time* manuscript. At the head of the list is Ray Simpson, Founding Guardian of the International Community of Aidan and Hilda, whom I regard as the number one scholar of the history and patterns of the ancient Celtic Church. My wife and I were privileged to spend a week with Ray on the Holy Isle of Lindisfarne in August 2019. What did that week do for me? It was like having a coloring book, with its black and white outlines, suddenly filled in with living color. I could not have written this book without that experience. And to top it all off, Ray was kind enough to read my manuscript and give me pointers.

I wish to thank Dr. David Rudolph, Director of Messianic Jewish Studies at The King's University in Southlake, Texas, for honoring me by reading and critiquing those parts of my manuscript that relate to Jewish history. I met David when he was Rabbi of Tikvat Israel in Richmond, not far from where I live. God gave us to become friends.

I also wish to thank Dr. Daniel Juster of Tikkun, International, for reading my manuscript and giving me much encouragement. Years ago, this man was my introduction to the Messianic Jewish world, which has been for me both worldview-changing and personally transformational.

Then I must add my thanks to Ann and Andy Franklin of Somerset, England, who have, time and again, come alongside me to offer me and my wife, Carla, help of all sorts. In this case, it was help evaluating my manuscript from an English point of view. They also opened the door for me to teach some of this material in Scotland in 2019.

Dr. Brad Long and Rev. Cindy Strickler, leaders of Presbyterian and Reformed Renewal Ministries, International, between the two of them, encouraged me to put my "Glory Through Time" teaching into book form. And, without them, I never would have had opportunities to start teaching this material in an international context.

My friend, Reuben Smith, encouraged me and previewed my manuscript. Without friends like this who believe in you, none of us would dare to do much of anything in this life!

Finally, may I acknowledge the encouragement given me by Fr. Ben Torrey, director of Jesus Abbey in Taebaek, Korea, who also happens to be the great-grandson of R. A. Torrey, the revivalist who did more than anyone to usher in the worldwide Revival of 120 years ago (as I will describe in Volume Two). Ben has not only been a source of primary material on the Korean Revival of 1907, but has been encouraging me in this "Glory Through Time" teaching for years. And thank you, Ben, for your foreword.

And through the revelation of the Anointed One, he un-
veiled his secret desires to us—the hidden mystery of his
long-range plan, which he was delighted to implement from
the very beginning of time. And because of God's unfail-
ing purpose, this detailed plan will reign supreme through
every period of time, until the fulfillment of all the ages
finally reaches its climax—when God makes all things new.

Ephesians 1:9-10 (The Passion Translation)

PREFACE

In 1983, I met Dick Simmons. He changed my life.

Before that moment, I identified myself as a Presbyterian pastor. After that moment, I began to identify myself as a citizen of the kingdom of God (while still being a pastor).

Dick described in detail the great spiritual awakenings of the past—those seasons when God showed up in His surprising and manifest power to transform cities, even whole nations. I had never heard such things. I was fascinated. Then hooked. I began to long for another such season to occur in my generation—a time when the kingdom of God would once again invade the nations of this world to transform them.

Since 1983, my wife, Carla, and I have devoted ourselves to praying for this. As we have done so, God has encouraged us by answering prayer in amazing ways. In 1985, in answer to prayer, God brought His judgment against the largest cult—Rajneeshpuram—that our nation has ever hosted. Today, the property belongs to Young Life.

Then in 1986, in answer to prayer, God dealt a blow to the spirit of murder in the city of Richmond, just when Richmond was experiencing the second-highest murder rate in the nation.

These answers to our first efforts at kingdom prayer were encouraging, to be sure. And yet to my mind, those displays of God's power were only warm-ups for the greatest of biblical promises (short of eternal life, and the return of the King), namely, that God would grant "a time of refreshing from the presence of the Lord" (Acts 3:19). This granddaddy of kingdom

1

promises lifted out of the apostle Peter's second sermon has been fulfilled perennially throughout the last 2000 years. In those seasons, the glory of the Presence seems to manifest itself more clearly than at other times.

When we began this type of prayer in 1983, few other Christians cherished this vision of "the next great awakening." Today, as I write this Preface, I am enjoying watching the gathering of hundreds of thousands of Americans on the Mall in Washington, DC, under the leadership of the Messianic Jewish rabbi, Jonathan Cahn, and under Franklin Graham, son of the famed evangelist, Billy Graham. These two gatherings held simultaneously on September 26, 2020, were an appeal to God to pour out His Spirit on our country once again—and to bring an end-time great awakening throughout the world. And prophecies were given that God is about to fulfill these great longings that God Himself has given us. How this hope and prayer has spread into the multitudes over the last thirty-five years!

And so, to encourage others to believe for, and pray for, another season of "great awakening," I have written *Glory Through Time* to review God's "times of refreshing" throughout the ages.

When people can see the awesome deeds of God in the past, they are much more likely to pray for God to do it again, as the prophet Habakkuk wrote:

> *Lord, I have heard of your fame;*
> *I stand in awe of your deeds, Lord.*
> *Repeat them in our day,*
> *In our time make them known.*
>
> *Habakkuk 3:2*

I like to say that my *Glory Through Time* narrative is "a track record of the kingdom of God." Some people don't like that expression, "the kingdom of God." It reminds them of many hurtful episodes when Christian faith was linked up with imperial power to damage whole races or nations, riding rough-shod over them in the name of Christ. I sympathize with this objection.

But these hurtful episodes only show a need to study the Gospel of the kingdom more closely. There is a stronghold of deception that entered the community of Christians in the fourth century. It began to twist the Gospel of the kingdom into something unrecognizable. If God said, "not by power nor by might but by My Spirit," this new teaching said just the opposite. Since it is the opposite of God's expressed desires, we call it a "stronghold" because it argues against the Word of God. (See 2 Corinthians 10:4-5 for Paul's definition of a stronghold.)

It was as though a virus had entered the Christian Church to take its breath away—and to twist the Body of Christ into horrible contortions. I have learned to call this twisted faith "Power-and-Might Christianity." This twisting of things eventually replaced the original By-My-Spirit kingdom as it had been introduced by King Jesus. To me, this is the greatest tragedy of Church history, a tragedy I will give my last breath to bring to an end.

And so, my story is partly a pathology of the kingdom of God. If God calls the Gospel of Jesus *The Gospel of the Kingdom* (i.e., Matthew 4:23), then surely it is not up to us to challenge His wording. It is better, I believe, to untwist this twisted thing we have made of it and try to rediscover the original intentions of God, which are always beautiful and good. We are the ones with messed-up thinking. Not God. Let us get more closely in touch with the thoughts of God if we want to get untwisted.

As I have studied the historic struggle between Power-and-Might Christianity and the original By-My-Spirit kingdom, I have come to a conclusion. The original untwisted version lasted roughly 700 years. After that—during the Middle Ages—the twisted version became normal among Christians. Then: the last 600-going-on-700 years have seen a steady but painfully slow return to the original pattern. This present volume traces the story of the first period when By-My-Spirit patterns still prevailed as normal. Surely we can learn some good lessons from the earlier times before the virus had caught on.

In this volume, I hope to tell the simple narrative of how God at first bestowed seven centuries of "times of refreshing from the presence of the Lord." During those years, the Gospel of the kingdom spread to the West all the way to Ireland. (It spread to the east, too, but that is not covered in this story.)

In Volume Two, I will show the renewal of the original patterns after a 700-year drought. It will take the form of the re-digging of ancient wells in the very same place that the original had so richly prospered—in Scotland. In Strathclyde, to be exact. From there, the very concept of "spiritual awakenings" would be birthed, and those would be the words—"spiritual awakening"—that future generations would use to describe that biblical promise of "times of refreshing from the presence of the Lord."

Those who read Volume One and would like an advance glimpse into the content of Volume Two may consult the "Glory Through Time" video teachings on my website, TheClearing.us. I have also turned these teachings into a podcast on iTunes (The

Clearing Podcast—Where Eagles Fly), and a YouTube channel (TheClearingMedia). You can also sign up for my monthly newsletter on my website; past issues of my newsletter become blog postings.

Glory Through Time, then, is a story of how Jesus, the By-My-Spirit King, has been overseeing the transformation of nations year by year and century by century—and how difficult it has been for us, who like to be in charge, to align ourselves with the thoughts of God.

—Doug McMurry, 2021

1

RELIGION VERSUS KINGDOM

God's thoughts are higher than our thoughts.

...And we, the human race, resent Him terribly for it.

Case in point: We are quite sure that Christianity is a religion. "One of the five great religions of the world." But from the start, God introduced Jesus as a king, not a religious leader. "He spoke as one who had authority and not as their scribes." And the Christian Gospel was given to us as "the Gospel of the kingdom." Not a religion. Does this not strike you as *unexpected?*

Yet: Is it really right, do you think, to say back to God, "I know you *said* 'kingdom.' But we all know you *meant*, 'religion.'" Is this not a good example of the very thing God once complained about:

For I knew how stubborn you were;
Your neck muscles were iron,
Your forehead was bronze.
Therefore I told you these things long ago;
Before they happened I announced them to you
So that you could not say,
"My images brought them about;
My wooden image and metal god ordained them?
From now on I will tell you of new things,
Of hidden things unknown to you."

Isaiah 48:4-6

The same prophet through whom God expressed these words of complaint also revealed God's plan for a coming king: And as we read through Isaiah, we get a surprisingly full picture of that king's life and kingdom, like snapshots from many different angles. Isaiah shows us what that King's kingdom will look like and how He will rule it. On earth as it is in heaven.

Maybe stubbornness doesn't exactly describe what's going on with us. The problem is that God's ways are so much higher than our ways. Human beings think humanly, while God thinks divinely. God has a knack for doing the unexpected. It irritates us, this way that God has.

But all of a sudden, one day, 2000 years ago, the thoughts of God took shape. God acted among us, like it or not. He did a completely new and divine thing, whether we were ready or not. And, sure enough, no one was ready.

We were too used to thinking the way humans always think. We have one idea for religions. Another for kingdoms. But what God decided to do didn't fit either category. So all of us have to look at what God *did* do, and we have to learn to adjust our thoughts and come up with new definitions of terms to fit a new reality. The kingdom of God.

Daniel

God's insistence on calling it a kingdom increased after Isaiah. Through the prophet Daniel, He prophesied the next four empires that were about to happen in world history after the sixth century BC. Then, He added, after those four empires will have come and gone (count them: Babylonian, Medo-Persian, Greek, Roman), He would send a *king* "whose kingdom will crush all those other kingdoms and bring them to an end, but it will itself endure forever" (Daniel 2:44). He insists on the word "kingdom" specifically by prophesying four world empires, which it will replace. And His thinking is amazingly consistent throughout the Bible: *A king*.

However, when the time came to actually send this king prior to the collapse of the Roman empire, we humans were so busy turning His kingdom into a religion that we failed to notice that He fulfilled His decreed promise right on schedule. Yes, Daniel 2:44 is a decree.

In the time of those kings the God of heaven will set up a kingdom that will never be destroyed, nor will it be left to another people. It will crush all those kingdoms and bring them to an end, but it will itself endure forever.

That's how kingdoms work. By decree.

The kingdom of God consists of the decrees and deeds of God. Religions, on the other hand, consist of decrees and deeds of *people on behalf of God*, building religious systems under human control. God wants us to know, by His word, that He was starting His kingdom, not so much a religion. Are we listening?

Magi

The Jews had called him Daniel, but the Persians had known him as Belteshazzar. This Jew had produced a cultural memory. Succeeding generations of Persians (today's Iranians) had regarded him as perhaps the greatest *rabmag* of all time. The *rabmag*, in case you are unfamiliar with the term, was head of the council of *magi*, the council who surrounded the king of

Persia and was responsible for counseling him with the wisdom of God. Belteshazzar had made no small mark in the history of the Babylonian and Medo-Persian empires, interpreting dreams and, like Isaiah, prophesying future empires. And as the world empires he prophesied came and went, successive generations of *magi* noticed that everything Belteshazzar had prophesied was taking place as decreed in advance by God.

And so we have the unlikely scenario of *magi* showing up in Jerusalem in the first century, enquiring after *a king*. A king? But the chief priests, who were supposed to look after these things for the Jews, didn't have a clue. They classed the prophetic writings as "poetry."[1]

The Wisdom of David

It could have been different. It could have been as it was in the days of King David, who refused to take the throne in Jerusalem until he had ensconced some of the sons of Aaron in the heart of Jerusalem, his capital city, doing what God wanted them to do: praising God, praying His prayers and prophesying His words. For as long as they were doing their part, pleasing the God of heaven, it was amazing how well things went in all the rest of David's realm. Battles. Harvests. Foreign relations. All that sort of thing.

But for them, it was not a religious system to be controlled and milked. It was a God to be loved, listened to, and honored night and day. Here was a good pattern: A king on His throne, humbly learning to listen to God; priests simultaneously prevailing in prayer and worship—the royal priesthood.

The contrast between that, in 1000 BC, and the religious system at the temple a thousand years later, made God's heart sick with grief. As expressed by King Yeshua:

*As he approached Jerusalem and saw the city, he wept over
it and said, "If you, even you had only known on this day
what would bring you peace—but now it is hidden from
your eyes."*

Luke 19:41-42

The New Testament Gospels tell the tragic story of the
blindness of the very religious leaders who were best equipped
to receive the King. Yet, when the King arrived among them,
many couldn't see Him.[2]

Significance of the Ascension

Most of us know the story of this King's death, His resurrection,
and His ascension to heaven "at the right hand of God." But
most of us fail to appreciate the last of these three events; we
usually focus on the first two alone.

However, to the early believers, the ascension of Jesus
was equally significant to the other two events because it
was the official beginning of the kingdom of God. That was
the day when Jesus actually did become King, according to
Belteshazzar the *rabmag*:

*In my vision at night I looked, and there before me was one
like a son of man, coming with the clouds of heaven. He
approached the Ancient of Days and was led into his presence.
He was given authority, glory and sovereign power; all
nations and peoples of every language worshiped him. His
dominion is an everlasting dominion that will not pass
away, and his kingdom is one that will never be destroyed.*

Daniel 7:13-14

The fact that we today so minimize the ascension that fulfilled this prophecy is one more indication that we do not comprehend the kingdom of God; we see only our religions.

Many are the biblical passages that speak of Jesus "coming on the clouds." We assume that these refer to His second coming. But most of them refer to this prophecy in Daniel, fulfilled by the ascension, which, as Jesus said, "some standing here will see" (Matthew 16:28). And so: "He was taken up before their very eyes, and a cloud hid him from their sight" (Acts 1:9). And the apostle John was given a vision of the significance of the ascension:

> *Then I looked and heard the voice of many angels, numbering thousands upon thousands, and ten thousand times ten thousand. They encircled the throne and the living creatures and the elders. In a loud voice they were saying: Worthy is the Lamb who was slain, To receive power and wealth and wisdom and strength And honor and glory and praise.*
>
> *Revelation 5:11-12*

It was the ascension, then, that marks the official beginning of the kingdom of God on earth, a kingdom that will demonstrate the decrees and the deeds of God Himself. Our story of the kingdom, therefore, will begin with what happened next, after the ascension described in Daniel 7:14, Acts 1:9, and Revelation 5—as the decrees and the deeds of a sovereign God began to manifest on the Day of Pentecost.

2

THE KINGDOM OF GOD, DAY ONE

The Day of Pentecost that occurred soon after the ascension of Jesus is almost always thought of as "the day God gave the Holy Spirit to the Church." But that is not what the apostles thought and taught. They taught that the events of that day were the fulfillment of ancient prophecy about the kingdom of God, which God had been announcing for centuries.

A kingdom, by nature, has to do with power (*dunamis*) and authority (*exousia*). Power of deed; authority of word. Yeshua (Jesus) became the King because He would be "more powerful than" John the Baptist—or anyone else, for that matter. Yet when Yeshua showed up in the temple in Jerusalem, they had swatted Him like a fly. He was no king!

But that was because, even though Yeshua was the prophesied King, His kingdom had not yet begun. Not quite. The King-in-waiting had not yet ascended "to the right hand of the Father," that is, to the place of power/authority. But then He told His little band to "wait in Jerusalem until you receive power from on high." And they did. Thank God. They listened and obeyed. And as a result, they became citizens of a new kingdom, full of power and authority.

It was Luke, the Greek physician turned Gospel-writer, who refused to let the written narrative end with a death and

13

a resurrection. Luke insisted on a story that included the full break-out of the kingdom of God, from death to resurrection to ascension to the manifest presence of the living God moving from the temple into the nations. It was Luke for whom this movement into the nations was the most relevant because he was not a Jew. His two-part narrative (the Gospel of Luke and the Acts of the Apostles) includes many stories gained by interviewing the Jews who were eye-witnesses, though he himself was neither Jew nor eye-witness. But he wanted to make sure everyone saw the flow from death to resurrection to ascension to the *Presence among the nations.*

A Fresh Look at Pentecost

As for the Galilean northerners, it could not have been comfortable for them to show up at the Court of the Gentiles for Shavuot, the Feast of Pentecost.[3] This was the very place where Yeshua had overturned the moneychangers' tables, the prophetic act that, more than any other, had set in motion the plot to destroy him.

The place was swarming with people from all over the diaspora wanting to celebrate the gift of the Torah on Mount Sinai. The 120, mostly from Galilee, were surely a cluster of country bumpkins in a sea of metropolitan splendor and confusion. Few of them particularly remembered that prophecy of 700 years before: "In the past He humbled the land of Zebulun and the land of Naphtali, But in the future He will honor Galilee of the Gentiles" (Isaiah 9:1).

Now, suddenly and without warning, there is a sound, heard by all, "like a mighty wind." It overpowers them so that every conversation is silenced, every ear strains to discover what is causing this sound. Then, there appears something like fire coming down from above and singling out these 120-or-so followers of Yeshua.[4] God is putting His seal of approval, publicly, on these believers from Galilee, in the presence of the crowds.

Then, an even more bizarre sign from God: the disciples of Yeshua are speaking out loud—yet other people around them hear them speaking, each one, in their own language. It is as though the King from heaven is declaring His intention to reverse the curse of the Tower of Babel! After that, God unleashes a wave of joy: people are breaking out in irrepressible laughter!

Of course, there would have to be some in the crowd who would attempt to trivialize all these signs and wonders. "Just drunks," they are mocking, even though it is obvious, there is more going on than what they are willing to see.

Whereupon Peter gains a place of visibility and opens his mouth to interpret for everyone why these things are happening. Quoting Joel 2, he proclaims that, starting today, God is ordaining a democracy of the Spirit. No longer will spiritual gifts be limited to prophets, priests, and kings, as before. God is going to begin distributing these anointings to lowborn, highborn, men, women, young, old—without distinction—beginning today.

These would not be easy words to speak, especially for someone with no theological training whatsoever. And you can imagine, for the hearers, it would seem that Peter is advocating a breakdown of order and decorum. As if that were not adequately risky, Peter then goes on to remind his fellow Jews that they are guilty of killing the long-awaited Messiah, whom God raised from the dead and gave Him the very power that is now being manifested before their eyes.

It is difficult to imagine people taking these words lying down. And yet...

The crowds are all suddenly cut to the heart! Peter's words have utterly demolished their self-composure. It is as though God Himself has smitten them with arrows of Truth. Peter seems to have authority with every word he speaks. *Exousia!* The authority of the King, flowing through Peter's mouth. And so, in spite of the weirdness, the inappropriate emotionalism, the mocking accusations, and the unimpressive demeanor of the preacher, 3000 Jews agree that everything Peter has just said is 100 percent true.[5] They repent! And they get baptized.

That's the kingdom of God. That's how it works. The result? Those Jewish disciples of the King turn themselves into a discipleship community to begin helping all these people follow King Yeshua. Obedience to His ways is of great importance to them precisely because He is King. The kingdom of God produces not a religion but discipleship: "teaching people to obey what I have commanded." The Church, in the beginning, is not a religious institution; it becomes, instantly, a discipleship community.

3

THE GATE BEAUTIFUL

Some days later, Peter and John are walking through the temple once again. It is possible that John was of the priestly class, and so he was much more familiar with the temple than Peter was. (This would explain why John was so well-known to the high priest Caiaphas, as we read in John 18:15. It would also explain why John so frequently demonstrates an intimate knowledge of the workings and significance of temple services in all his later writings.[6]) John will spend the rest of his life describing the kingdom of God in terms of the temple and its services. John himself is about to witness it: The manifest presence of God, which has been physically located in the Holy of Holies, is now going *to move out to the nations!* It is as though—can it be?—all who follow Yeshua (Jesus) are actually invited to become priests?[7]

John would one day explain it this way:

> *To him who loves us and has freed us from our sins by his blood, and has made us to be a kingdom and priests to serve his God and Father—to him be glory and power for ever and ever! Amen!*

> *Revelation 1:5, 6*

Eventually, Peter would express it this way:

As you come to him, the living Stone—rejected by humans but chosen by God and precious to him—you also, like living stones, are being built into a spiritual house to be a holy priesthood, offering spiritual sacrifices acceptable to God through Jesus Christ.

1 Peter 2:4-5

But I am getting ahead of my story.

John and Peter are climbing the steps that lead from the south wall of the temple complex (from the direction of the City of David and the Tomb of Huldah) to emerge into the hustle and bustle in the middle of the Court of the Gentiles. Here they see the money-changers' tables, once again doing a brisk business. They are walking toward the right, past crowds of people and bleating animals, to Solomon's Porch, with its ancient columns, the only part of the original Temple of Solomon that remained standing after the Babylonian debacle. From Solomon's Porch, they turn left to enter the Court of Women, where the Jewish public is meant to enter for services.

The temple is designed to lead from one area to the next in a succession of "rooms." Each "room" or court requires you to go up some steps, and the steps mark a delineation that excludes someone. Once Peter and John are in the Court of Women, no Gentile can follow.

Here are located the thirteen treasure chests of the temple treasury, each shaped like a brass trumpet with a wide mouth at the top, each one carefully labeled, to indicate which type of donation should be placed there.

(People would throw their shekels in the mouth, the money clattering down the brazen throat and landing with a clank in the chest. This may be what Jesus meant by "sounding the trumpet when you give alms.") Here too, were brass plaques honoring those wealthy businessmen who had given their entire inheritance to the Temple, thus leaving their widows penniless, for which Jesus again denounced temple leaders for "devouring widows' houses."

The Weightiest of Doors

Let us follow Peter and John west across this courtyard to the next set of steps that lead into the Israel Court, where the animal sacrifices are offered on the massive Altar of Unhewn Stones. At the top of these steps is a pair of doors of dazzling beauty, covered entirely in Corinthian brass, doors so massive and tall that it requires twenty strong men to open them each morning and close them each evening.

At the entrance to this impressive passageway, the Sanhedrin has given permission for a particular lame man to beg for alms day after day. No one knows why he has gained such favor with the powers that be, but everyone who has passed through these gates to do any business with God in the Israel Court would recognize this man. No doubt he is the most famous, recognizable beggar in all Jerusalem. As Peter and John are passing up the steps into the Israel Court, this beggar holds out his cup expectantly, even though Peter and John look to be as poor as—well, Galilean fishermen.

Peter is suddenly struck with that now-familiar awareness that the Triune God is there in an extraordinary way and is about to do something. He looks intently at the man, staring into his hopeful eyes. Then he speaks those fateful words, loaded with significance (considering the locale they have just passed through): "Silver and gold have I none, but what I have, I give to you."

Suddenly, the man's limbs grow out, get themselves untwisted, and become completely normal! God has contrived a powerful act that will instantly be recognized without question by every single person who sees it. It immediately gains the attention of everyone in the Court of Women, including the women in the galleries on three sides, the men streaming up the steps into the Israel Court, the people throwing donations into the temple treasury, and, yes, the chief priests who happen to be monitoring the whole business.

It is as though Yeshua Himself is there! Not dead after all. Through some mysterious metamorphosis, He is just as present there in the temple as if He had never died. For most of them, this is good news. For some, it is not. Jesus has become a powerful King. Everyone now has to deal with this new reality. Like it or not.

A Sign of the Presence

Strictly speaking, the creative "miracle" of the healing of lame legs was not a miracle at all but a *sign*. A miracle is a work of wonder that draws attention to itself. A "sign" is a wonderful work designed to point to a deeper, unseen reality—like a road sign at the side of the road pointing to a curve in the road. God is using a sign to point further up and further on to His unseen *Presence*.

For centuries, God had bestowed His manifest Presence in the Holy of Holies. But several weeks or months prior to that day, the temple curtain in that inner sanctum had torn from top to bottom—another sign, which surely had confounded the Sanhedrin, who must have wondered at the ominous meaning of it all. (And, of course, they were the ones charged with repairing the damage.)

Now, it is as though the *Presence* is emerging from the Holy of Holies, emerging even from the Holy Place on the other side of the curtain, crossing the Israel Court with its altar for burnt offerings, meeting Peter and John at the Gate Beautiful, and carrying the crowd out of the Court of Women and back into Solomon's Porch. The healing of the lame man is thus a sign of something far greater and truly momentous that is happening before their very eyes. The Presence of God is moving!

The sight of this lame man walking and leaping is so astonishing that everyone within sight of him immediately forms themselves into a crowd, which departs the Court of Women, leaving it empty, and gathers itself on the steps of Solomon's Portico. Peter knows that the King is once again looking to him to explain the meaning of it all. He opens his mouth, and out comes a complete, succinct explanation of the kingdom of God, the clearest and most cogent description of God's intentions for the human race that we have in our Bibles or anywhere else.

Peter is telling them (and us) that human history is now to be divided into two parts, a "now" part and a "then" part. For now, there are to be "times of refreshing from the presence of the Lord" (verse 19).[8] That is how the kingdom of God will operate for an undisclosed period of the history of nations. (And there goes that presence, out to the nations, even as Peter was saying the words!)

But at a point known only to God, human history will move suddenly into Stage Two, the "then" part. At that point, the King will return to this world. The purpose of this second advent will be not to whisk the Church away into heaven but to "restore all things" (verse 21). This restoration will complete God's plans for His kingdom. Both parts of this story have the same objective: to make heaven and earth to be completely one so that there is no distinction, no separation between the two. "On earth as it is in heaven."

By becoming King, Yeshua (Jesus) has embraced the task of ultimately producing this transformation. If we Christians are followers of King Jesus, we will embrace that task as well. It is our task because it is His task. We will align ourselves with the destiny of the King. As kingdom citizens, this becomes our new goal, our new personal destiny. And our new identity. We are restorers working for the transformation of this world under the authority of King Jesus. By His power and by His authority.

The real problem is this: All of humanity has become lame, and all of our relationships are crippled. People are in torment. Nations are at war. The human race is sick with virus.

But: Jesus has now become our King, and His kingdom, starting from the Gate Beautiful on the Temple Mount, is going to begin to heal that lameness in all peoples.

It is now time to take a hard look at the lameness of Rome— that crippled "fourth" Empire that Daniel, alias Belteshazzar, had prophesied about in Daniel 2:44. It is there that we will begin to examine the distinction between a kingdom and a religion. And we can thank God that He gave us, not a religion, but a very transformational kingdom.

4

THE LAMENESS OF ROME

Why would God establish His kingdom at the precise moment when He did, to coincide with the decline and fall of the Roman Empire? What was happening at the time to cause Him to choose that occasion for the birthing of His kingdom? Let me draw for you a picture of a God who sees a world sliding into despair and who provides for people a genuine hope to pull them out of that despair. (The world is in just such a state now; have you noticed?)

The Roman Empire had a hope; it followed a cherished vision statement. Rome was going to be a republic. The republic was going to be infused with enlightened philosophy—Stoic philosophy, moral philosophy. Then Rome, the civilized republic, would conquer all the barbaric peoples around them and impose their higher ways in successively widening circles of civilization until the whole world would become civilized. That was the plan.

The key to civilized Roman society was the *pater familias*, an orderly way for all Romans to grow up into adulthood in which men would be in authority, faithful to their wives, raising good, stable, loving, peaceful families to build a stable and civilized society. This society would be presided over by a senate, in which enlightened leaders would discuss what was good for Rome as a whole. This seemed like a good way to do things.

Except that it didn't work out that way.

The most enlightened senators knew that they needed to avoid sliding into tyranny. But slide is what they did. In 49 BC, Julius Caesar came back from conquering the Celts of Gaul. (He conquered them by killing vast numbers of them.) This victorious general was so popular (with Romans, not Celts), they couldn't seem to keep him from being a virtual emperor. This was not supposed to happen. The "executive branch" was supposed to consist of three rulers, all subject one to another out of mutual respect, like philosopher kings, cheerfully working together.

But as it turned out, the Caesar family, forming themselves into a dynasty and sated with lust for power, became increasingly uncivilized with the passing of the generations. It is a sad story, but let me tell it anyway. It is relevant for us.

Augustus Caesar

Octavian and his wife, Livia, who followed Julius in the line of succession, attempted to live up to the image of Roman virtue that Rome expected of them. Octavian ("Augustus Caesar") made a point of not flaunting his power, even though, technically, he was the first true Emperor, who didn't have to share power with anyone else. By the time of his rule, Rome had had it with triumvirates. Shared power hadn't worked out so well. So now, they were going to have to be comfortable with a dictator, and Octavian was a successful one. "I found a city of brick and left it one of marble," he summarized at the end of his reign.

Tiberius Caesar

Things went seriously off track with the next generation, however. Octavian's daughter, Julia, turned out to have no sense of morals whatsoever. Adultery was her middle name; she flaunted unfaithfulness to the point that all Rome was aflame with gossip. Not only that, Octavian ordered his step-son (by his wife's previous marriage), Tiberius, to marry Julia for the sake of the dynasty. Tiberius had already married a woman he loved (Vipsania), and the order to divorce her to marry his step-sister, a woman known for her adulteries, broke his heart. Tiberius was now in a relationship with a woman he loathed, supposedly for "the good of Rome." This was a formula for disaster.

Looking for an escape from all this, Tiberius created for himself a pleasure palace on the Isle of Capri. At this island paradise, he gave himself over to every sexual pleasure he could think of. Becoming a sex addict, he trained little boys to dress up like gods, and entice him into their lairs, etc., etc. You get the idea. This man made Jeffrey Epstein look like a Sunday School teacher by comparison. A man utterly cynical toward women, cavorting with little boys.

While he was away, he gave the rulership of Rome to the Prefect of the Praetorian Guard, Sejanus. This fit Sejanus' plans perfectly. He used the opportunity to try to work Tiberius out of the picture entirely. Tiberius was clueless, vacationing on his pleasure island for months at a time.

One by one, Sejanus tortured and killed Tiberius' potential successors. Agrippina, the daughter of Julia, was incarcerated for years. After one beating, she lost an eye. When she tried to take her life by starving herself to death, she was violently force-fed. Not until four years later would she be allowed to waste away, leaving behind her youngest son, Gaius Julius Caesar, or "Caligula."

Finally, Tiberius was alerted to what was happening back in Rome. He rushed back to discover Sejanus' treason and took action. He not only had Sejanus put to death but initiated a great purge of Roman leadership.

> *The Roman "justice" system had become a killing machine. Those convicted were grabbed with a sharp iron hook and dragged to the top of the Gemonian Steps to be strangled before being hurled down, still gasping and twitching, to be finished off by the crowd, then simply left to rot. One day saw no fewer than twenty of these state-sponsored lynchings. By law, it was forbidden for virgins to be strangled. Scrupulously, then, the executioner would rape any maiden who fell into his hands before continuing with his work in the usual way.[9]*

Before Tiberius died (seven years later), he chose his successor, Caligula, and mentored him in the delights of his vacation spot on Capri.

Caligula

Caligula was one of those irresistible children who gain a reputation for cuteness. Becoming a kind of army mascot, soldiers would dress him up like a little soldier from head to foot and parade him before the army. The name *Caligula*, "Little Boots," had been given him at a young age by fawning soldiers, and it stuck. Everyone thought he was adorable. Then he became Emperor.

Who would have dreamed there could be an emperor worse than Tiberius? Caligula soon learned that, as Emperor, he was now empowered to do whatever his heart desired. So he immediately brought to Rome all the entertainments and pastimes that had been hidden away on the Isle of Capri. He would hold banquets, to which he invited the great leaders of Rome and their wives. Then he would choose a wife from this august assembly, take her into a back room, have sex, then come back into the banquet hall and report on his escapade to all his guests, rating the woman on how "good" she was. Of course, no one liked to attend these banquets. But making excuses to Little Boots was risky business. In this way, the young Emperor began to grow a garden of enemies among the leading families of the aristocracy.

Tiberius had been a frugal tyrant, storing up two billion sesterces for government projects. Little Boots spent all that in just his first year, most of it on silliness. He built a three-mile bridge by putting two rows of cargo ships end-to-end, then covering them with dirt, forming a road so that he and his Praetorian Guard could ride back and forth across it.

On the Palatine Hill, he erected a life-size statue of himself, covered it in gold, then ordered that it be clothed each day with whatever type of clothing he happened to be wearing. Then he decided to use the temple in Jerusalem for his personal Emperor cult. (Herod Agrippa persuaded him to change his plans just in time to avoid a major "Jewish" crisis.)

After four years of this sort of thing, the people of Rome had had enough. On January 17 in the year 41, his haters triumphed, killing him while he attended a theatrical performance. And that was the end of him.

But the people of Rome who remembered the original vision of civilized society were now wondering if they had not somehow created a beast: a monster called "Rome."

Claudius

Then came Claudius, Caligula's uncle, next in the Caesar line (because Caligula had killed all the others). Claudius was as opposite to Caligula as could be imagined.

> *From boyhood, he had been sickly and physically not entirely in control. His hands shook, he stammered, he had a tendency to drool and he lurched and limped in an awkward manner when he tried to walk. He would burst out laughing, abruptly and unaccountably. He would fly into rages, spitting and slobbering as he raved.*[10]

Despite the fact that he had been ridiculed by almost everyone for what would today be called a handicap or a "challenge," Claudius did manage to function as a fairly decent ruler. His problem came from his marriages. It was now the women's turn to be monstrous.

> *Claudius' third wife, Valeria Messalina, was a truly terrifying woman: murderous in her rages, insatiable in her lusts. Those who resisted her sexual advances or crossed her in any other way quickly found themselves paying for their temerity with their lives.*[11]

Valeria Messalina was a one-woman sexual revolution. She insisted on coming out of the closet with whatever sexual urge happened to overpower her on any given day. One day, she challenged the most renowned prostitute of Rome to a sexual endurance contest. (She won.)After that, she staged a public "wedding" between herself and her lover, Gaius Silius, despite the fact that both were already married—and she to the Emperor of Rome! It was important to Madame Messalina that she be permitted the freedom to "be herself," and she refused to be ashamed of who she was, an adulteress of the first order. The cuckolded Emperor found this public humiliation too much and reluctantly ordered his third wife put to death. Apparently, he was of an older generation of prudes.

Then came his fourth wife, Agrippina. This Agrippina, who knew how to manipulate Claudius to her every whim, was Claudius' niece. In her new position as wife, she persuaded Claudius to adopt her son into the Imperial family. She also contrived to get her son married to Claudius' daughter just for good measure. Her one object in all this incestuous scheming was to make sure that her son ended up being the next Emperor.

Nero

And that is how Nero became Emperor of Rome, the last in the dynasty of Julius Caesar. By now, the good families of Rome were desperate for even the smallest shred of hope that they could still be a civilized empire. So they attached to Nero the most famous Stoic philosopher of the day: Seneca, whose job was to school Nero so that he wouldn't end up like Tiberius, Caligula, or Claudius. Seneca was supposed to produce a civilized emperor.

Growing up under a completely domineering mother, Nero adopted an effeminate lifestyle in appearance and dress, then quickly became the top "alternative lifestyles" Emperor of all time. Utterly bi-sexual, he paraded his new type of morality in public, sometimes with men, sometimes with women.

Feeling smothered by his mother Agrippina, he contrived to have her killed. In the last viewing of her body, he laid her out completely naked, coldly declaring, "I never knew I had such a beautiful mother." Whatever restraints he had felt in his behaviors under her influence now vanished, and from then on, he became truly monstrous.

In the year 64, a great fire devoured most of downtown Rome. Of the city's fourteen districts, only four remained untouched. Hundreds of people died. Looters roamed the city.

> *Not that Nero was bothered. Notoriously, he went up to the palace roof, where the views were better, then sang, as he strummed cheerfully on his lyre. The song he performed, the "Capture of Troy," commemorated another great city's destruction.*[12]

Some historians (like Tacitus) have tried to defend Nero, claiming that he was nowhere around at the time. But the people of Rome themselves would have none of it. When they saw his response to the great fire, they knew! Nero gleefully cleared away all the charred rubble and began work on his cherished project—the *Domus Aurea*, The Golden House, which he had already been planning for months.

> *It was a truly monumental folly, the insanity starting in the vast vestibule with a colossal statue of Nero himself. Behind a triple colonnade well over half a mile long was a complex of buildings. These were laid out in the form of miniature cities, clustered around a lake made up with sandy shores and inlets like a sea.*[13]

This "Golden House" turned out to be three hundred structures, built on top of 300 acres. Suetonius tells us that the main dining hall was a circular room designed to turn constantly, day and night, like the heavens.

Nero wanted himself to become the new moral standard, and he used The Golden House for that purpose, to train Rome to live like himself.

> *There some of the city's most aristocratic virgins and wives were to be found, along with the capital's most glamorous courtesans. However respectable, they were under orders not to turn down any approach on pain of death. A more outrageous affront to the social proprieties can hardly be imagined, especially because there were male slaves among the Emperor's guests, allowed to have their pick of the patrician women. Senators and consuls could only look on helplessly as their wives were raped, their daughters deflowered by slaves and gladiators.*[14]

At the same time all this was happening, Nero found himself being blamed for the great fire that had cleared away the area for his Golden House. His answer? Blame the Christians. And so, to provide himself with a scapegoat, he contrived the first massive, systematic persecution of Christians in the history of the world. He would have Christians arrested, tie them to posts at the entrances of Rome and turn them into human torches just as dignitaries were riding by to important meetings in the city. And so, the kings of barbarian countries soon got a taste of what civilized Rome had become.

Death of the Dream

Nero surely takes the prize as the worst Emperor Rome ever had, though there would be plenty of other candidates later on. In the end, he committed suicide in 68 AD (as his tutor Seneca had already done). A dream died with him, the dream of a civilized Rome, as did the Julio-Claudian dynasty itself. Future emperors found the Golden House an embarrassment, and none chose to live there. It became an empty ghetto, then a ghost town, after Nero's death. Eventually, it was dismantled, and other buildings (like the Colosseum) were built over it.[15]

There were those who hoped the moral disaster of Rome was merely due to the Julian dynasty, so they chose other dynasties to rule the Empire. For a time, it looked as though they might succeed—in the days of Marcus Aurelius, who was Emperor from 161 to 180. Here was a "philosopher king," the very epitome of good emperors, according to the original vision of Roman rulers. But Marcus was so disgusted with what Rome had become that he preferred to stay away from the city he ruled, riding out on military adventures hither and yon.

But then his son, Commodus, took his place (some said Commodus poisoned his father). The son absolutely loved what Rome had become. Historian Susan Wise Bauer describes the result:

> *His misdeeds after that became the stuff of legend. He assembled an equal-opportunity harem of three hundred women and three hundred boys; he insisted on fighting in gladiatorial games, dressed as a gladiator himself; he murdered one of his sisters and forced another to sleep with him; he walked around Rome wearing "women's dress and lionskin," striking down citizens with a club.*[16]

The film "Gladiator" really doesn't do him justice. He was much more insanely wicked than Hollywood portrayed him.

Most people today choose not to look into the gross darkness that enveloped the Roman Empire during the years the Messiah walked the earth. We like to cherish a more benign picture of ancient Rome because that fonder picture nurtures similar hopes for our own plans to be civilized. The truth of what Rome actually became puts a serious damper on our own fond hopes for a civilized human race. Sometimes the truth hurts.

Can we see more clearly now why God had already made a decree?—not to combine the Roman Empire with the kingdom of God in a new hybrid combination of the two. No, what God had decreed was to turn to a completely different power source that God revealed through His Son—and begin building His kingdom with that new power, the Holy Spirit. His kingdom was to "crush" the Roman Empire and all other empires like it. Crush them and replace them. Clear the boards and start over.

But then, well, people had "a better idea."

5

THE BY-MY-SPIRIT PATTERN

Let me push *pause* here for just a minute to define more clearly what I mean by "the kingdom of God." God was being utterly creative when He established this kingdom and, even though it was not "of this world," it was still *on this earth*. It was a power sent among the nations, which was to transform them by making possible a new pattern to be lived out, by the power of God coming in a new way. This was real power, and people could soon see that it was changing things dramatically. The kingdom of God was and is a transforming power. It is a power that opens up a new pattern of life, which I call the "By-My-Spirit" pattern. So let's look at that pattern in this chapter before moving on with our story.

The By-My-Spirit Pattern
There is, then, a seven-fold pattern that seems to emerge quite consistently throughout the ages. Whenever the power of God manifests, it results in this pattern re-emerging. Identifying the ingredients of this pattern will help us identify by contrast the alternative twisting of things that appeared in the fourth century, which I call Power-and-Might Christianity. What does it mean, then, when we call this King the "By-My-Spirit" King to fulfill the prophecy of Zechariah 4:6?

The following seven ingredients form a common pattern that will characterize the kingdom of God in every future age. So, when we speak of the advance of the kingdom, these are the ingredients that will spread in all directions from Jerusalem. Especially, I will trace them through the Egyptian desert, north into Gaul, and then into the British Isles, until they will bump against the Atlantic Ocean. Here are the seven ingredients of "By-My-Spirit" Christianity.

1. Surrender to the King. The kingdom of God begins with an act of surrender. If Jesus is King, then *we are not*. Like the knights of old, kneeling before their king, there was a pledge of loyalty, a submission to His will. "For whoever wants to save their life will lose it, but whoever loses their life for me will find it. What good will it be for someone to gain the whole world yet forfeit their soul? Or what can anyone give in exchange for their soul?" (Matthew 16:25-26) Self-surrender is where it begins, symbolized by baptism.

2. Ask for the Holy Spirit. The Holy Spirit is essential equipment for the journey. "If you, then, though you are evil, know how to give good gifts to your children, how much more will your Father in heaven give the Holy Spirit to those who ask him!" (Luke 11:13) Faith is more than a set of doctrines. It is a walk of trust, an openness to the promises of the King. In the New Testament, sometimes the "asking" part is implied; but the Holy Spirit, like all the promises of God, is "received by faith" (Galatians 3:5). And that means asking in faith so that we can tap into the powerful methods of God.

3. <u>Let God Write His Laws on Our Hearts.</u> Perhaps the most important role of the Holy Spirit is to cause us to want righteousness and purity of heart. "Unless I go away, the Advocate will not come to you; but if I go, I will send him to you. When he comes, he will prove the world to be in the wrong about sin and righteousness and judgment: about sin, because people do not believe in me; about righteousness, because I am going to the Father, where you can see me no longer; and about judgment, because the prince of this world now stands condemned" (John 16:7-11). The prophets had said that the day was coming when God would "put my law in their minds and write it on their hearts" (Jeremiah 31:33). This is part of the process of "restoring" that Jesus accomplishes during the present age. It involves the transformation of character over time. This is a central feature in all spiritual awakenings.

4. <u>Humility and Servanthood</u> result from this process. The Holy Spirit is constantly setting Jesus before our eyes, who "left us an example that we should follow in His steps." Jesus was incarnate among us for this purpose, and we cannot get out from under the force of His humility. Is the servant greater than his master? Of course not.

5. <u>Love and Unity</u> in turn result from humility, and cannot prosper without it. "Be completely humble and gentle; be patient, bearing with one another in love. Make every effort to keep the unity of the Spirit through the bond of peace" (Ephesians 4:1-2). "Therefore if you have any encouragement from being united with Christ, if any comfort from his love, if any common sharing in the Spirit, if any tenderness and compassion, then make my joy complete by being like-minded, having the same love, being one in spirit and of one mind.

Do nothing out of selfish ambition or vain conceit. Rather, in humility value others above yourselves" (Philippians 2:1-3). Christian love and unity grow up in a garden fertilized by humility, modeled by Jesus the incarnate King. No exceptions.

6. The Authority of Prayer is the authority that Jesus gives us to advance the kingdom of God throughout the earth. Jesus shares His divine authority as we learn surrender, reliance on the Holy Spirit, purity of heart, humility in relationships, and unity in the Body of Christ. The kingdom of God is all about authority—how we get it, how we use it. "To the one who is victorious and does my will to the end, I will give authority over the nations—that one will rule them with an iron scepter and will dash them to pieces like pottery—just as I have received authority from my Father" (Revelation 2:26-27).

7. None of this is possible apart from a Direct Connection with God, which was made possible for all believers by the death of the King. We waste that death if we never make use of the connectedness that He bought for us. "Therefore, brothers and sisters, since we have confidence to enter the Most Holy Place by the blood of Jesus, by a new and living way opened for us through the curtain, that is, his body, and since we have a great priest over the house of God, let us draw near to God with a sincere heart and with the full assurance that faith brings, having our hearts sprinkled to cleanse us from a guilty conscience and having our bodies washed with pure water" (Hebrews 10:19-22). All else flows from this basic reality of prayer that approaches God.

This seven-part understanding of what Christianity is and how it works remained the prevailing lifestyle for Christians for centuries—"the pattern of sound teaching." With these seven ingredients, I have tried to describe the essence of what is going to emerge again and again during the "times of refreshing from the presence of the Lord" that Peter prophesied—right up to the present day.

ƀ

THE VILLAIN OF THE STORY

As we examine how Acts 3:19 will be fulfilled throughout the centuries, we must recognize that there is a villain in the story. Real life has villains. Let us not tell the story as though the kingdom of God advances easily, without opposition. At first, the opposition came from pagans. But then...

While the Pause button is still down, let me take you to consider the Big Picture for a moment. I don't want you to misunderstand who this villain is. When we set our eyes not on our churches but on God's presence through the ages, we will see human history differently than Church history buffs do. Denominations and religious traditions fade into the background as soon as we adjust our eyes to the brightness of God's manifest Presence. It turns out that God is willing to use Christian people from all of the churches; He is amazingly tolerant, free of preferences. Other realities emerge, which become much more important. For example, the "By My Spirit" pattern described in the previous chapter becomes more important.

In the past, sometimes, Christians have looked at other denominations as villains. That is not the sort of villain I will be describing here.

Most of our historic denominations emerged during seasons of God's presence. Great awakenings produced most of the old-line denominations. During "times of refreshing," new generations became fascinated with and transformed by the Presence. I am showing you just such a season of power in these pages. Thousands responded to the Presence of the King, and, behold, new churches emerged. This pattern continues to this day.

Begin in the Spirit; End in the Flesh
Eventually, however, two or three generations pass, and people forget what it was like to encounter the very Presence of God. In time, a movement fueled by the Presence turns itself into a religious institution. I see this pattern over and over through the centuries. It matters not what the denomination or church label might be. It is as though, after a time, in each case, a virus enters in and drains the life from this vibrant community who started out encountering God. Why? How do churches lose the Presence? Perhaps we can come up with some answers to this question as we tell the story of the Times of Refreshing throughout the centuries. What is this virus that enters in to rob the Body of Christ of the Breath of God?

The virus is consistent throughout the centuries. It operates by predictable patterns. We can study it as it attacks the lungs of the Body of Christ, trying to take its breath away.

And yet, we have seemed ill-equipped to diagnose this sickness, even though it persists, and it operates in a predictable way. So let me try at least to give it a name as we examine its effects over the centuries. I call this virus "Power-and-Might Christianity." The result of the virus is that Christian people have trouble catching their breath—or rather, catching God's breath. A virus has stolen in and taken away the Breath of the Body of Christ. Is this a curable disease?

For a while, people do not notice the problem. All seems well. We carry on as always. But in time, we all begin to notice: life has drained out of our fellowships. The Presence of God is no longer among us. We have become, merely, a collection of religious traditions that we are trying to keep alive. Behold, the Christian Church has become a religious institution! What happened to the kingdom of God? Our Gospel used to be the Gospel of the kingdom? What happened to turn it into a religion?

And in the process, too, each of the seven ingredients described in the previous chapter becomes twisted until they, all of them, become unrecognizable. Power-and-Might patterns have taken over, replacing the original By-My-Spirit patterns. All seven of them, as one.

But God...
Yet, God Himself has declared His intention, leaving no room for misunderstanding: "Not by power, nor by might, but by my Spirit, says the Lord" (Zechariah 4:6).

And when Jesus appeared among us, He walked out the By-My-Spirit patterns, as did the apostles and the apostolic fathers of the Church after them. For seven hundred years, these were the normal patterns lived out by Christians. After all, it is what Jesus and the apostles had taught, and it was the teaching of the Word, as we shall see in these pages. Most Christians to the west of Jerusalem still held to By-My-Spirit teaching, right up to the end of that 700-year period.

But in the fourth century, a new pattern was introduced, a Power-and-Might infection. By the eighth century, it will have spread to the point that Power-and-Might Christianity becomes the normal and expected pattern for most Christians. So let me tell you that story if I can—how the Power-and-Might virus first began to infect the Church. Not a person. Not a denomination. A disease.

And from then on, there will be a new villain in the picture right up to the present day, creating havoc in the kingdom of God. A disease that resists the Presence.

When the Last Apostle Died

With the Pause button still pressed down, let me make one final small observation. For many years, growing up as a Christian, I heard it stated repeatedly that God "withdrew the gifts of the Spirit" or "stopped doing miracles" long ago. These changes in the plan of God were alleged to have happened "when the last apostle died" or "once the Bible was completed." If you have been around Christians for any length of time, I feel sure that you have heard someone or other make such claims. It is a common belief.

And yet, I have often felt that, if it were true, there would be some evidence for this thing that God is alleged to have stopped doing. In other words, as we look to this very period of time (when the last apostle died at the end of the first century, or when the Bible came into being in the second and third centuries), we ought to be able to verify this claim historically, shouldn't we? So this is a side-issue that we can check out as the story of the kingdom of God is told.

Well, enough said for now. I'm not going to say anything more about this but simply tell the story of what God did do. Did God *stop* doing something during these centuries? Judge for yourself.

Now, back to our story.

Ƶ

A New Alliance

The Roman Church, more than any others, had to bear the heaviest burden of persecution in the early years. Malachi Martin, a Roman Catholic writer whom I will quote often in this chapter, describes the experience of Pontian, one of the popes during those years:

> Pontian was picked up by Maximinus's guards on that September 27, 235, and thrown into Mamertine Prison. The next day, the sixty-seven-year-old Pontian abdicated in favor of a man called Anterus, who automatically became pope according to accepted custom. In the meanwhile, the seventy-year-old Hippolytus, as a long-standing and prominent Christian, was also arrested, on September 29, and immediately shipped off to the lead mines on Sardinia. Back in Rome, Pontian was tortured for about ten days in the hope that he would inform on other Christian leaders (he did not), and then he too was condemned to the Sardinian mines, where he arrived about October 12.
>
> ...Here they were all—men and women—properly inducted as slave miners: the left eye was gouged out with a dagger and the socket cauterized with molten iron; the

joints of the left foot were burnt; and one nerve at the back of the right knee was sliced.

All males under thirty years were castrated. Then, when all had been branded with a number on the forehead, each one was manacled in the slave-miners' fashion: iron rings were soldered around the ankles and linked together by a six-inch chain; then a tight chain was placed around the waist (prisoners lost weight rapidly, so the chain had to catch at the hip-bones); this chain was attached by a third chain to the ankle-chain in such a way that the prisoner could never straighten up again. He had to bend down anyway for twenty out of the twenty-four hours per day. No locks were used; all chains were soldered permanently.[17]

The Roman Christians saw, more clearly than anyone, what a lie the whole vision of "Roman civilization" was. Behind the pretense of civilization lay a barbarity equal to any barbarian nations of the time.

Rags to Riches Overnight

But then, in 313 AD, something happened that changed everything. Changed the relationship between the Empire and the Church. Constantine became Emperor of Rome and released the Christian Church from persecution. By the Edict of Milan properties of Christians that had been stolen by the Empire under Diocletian were actually returned to their rightful owners! Now there was a friend on the Roman throne, and the Edict of Milan proved it. Under the new Emperor, the Church went from rags to riches almost overnight.

From Constantine's point of view, it was a mutual benefit. Emperor Diocletian, who had been responsible for massive cruelty towards Christians, decided to retire in 305, before his own death, so that he could help monitor the transfer of power. In the confusion that resulted in an unstable season for the Empire, Constantine saw an opportunity for himself to pull the Empire together under himself. As he began to imagine a way for himself to merge a tetrarchy so that the entire Empire would come under his own power, an event happened, described by Eusebius*:

A most marvelous sign appeared to him from heaven, the account of which it might have been hard to believe had it been related by any other person. But since the victorious emperor himself long afterwards declared it to the writer of this history, when he was honored with his acquaintance and society, and confirmed his statement by an oath, who could hesitate to accredit the relation…? He said that about noon, when the day was already beginning to decline, he saw with his own eyes the trophy of a cross of light in the heavens, above the sun, and bearing the inscription, Conquer by this. At the sight he himself was struck with amazement.… (W)hile he continued to ponder and reason on its meaning, night suddenly came on; then in his sleep the Christ of God appeared to him with the same sign which he had seen in the heavens, and commanded him to make a likeness of that sign which he had seen in the heavens, and to use it as a safeguard in all engagements with his enemies.[18]

---

*All grammar and spelling have been left unedited.

Constantine challenged Maxentius, his competitor for the throne of the western part of the Empire, at the Milvian Bridge on the Tiber River. He had his soldiers paint the Chi-Rho, the first two Greek letters in the word "Christ" on their shields.[19] Though Maxentius had a larger army, Constantine turned them back. In attempting to cross back over the Tiber River, many were drowned, including Maxentius himself. This victory at the Battle of Milvian Bridge gave Constantine control over the western half of the Empire. It was just a matter of time before he managed to unite the entire Empire under his headship. And he credited his success to Jesus Christ and his newfound faith.

This was huge. And it would be easy to believe that suddenly God had engineered a complete change of atmosphere over the whole "civilized" world of the Roman Empire. But Malachi Martin, the Roman Catholic writer I will rely on for my description of what followed, sees a looming problem here as he describes what happened next. Let me summarize his vivid ten-page description of Constantine's first encounter with the leaders of the Roman Church.

Constantine Forms an Alliance

On a quiet *corsia* in Rome, the massive presence of Constantine shows up, with all his retinue in tow, seeking out the hidden apartment of Pope Miltiades. Miltiades, the undersized, dark-skinned Pope, a humble man of Berber blood, has spent most of his days avoiding government employees, trying his best to be left alone. (Government attention never led to anything good.) Haltingly, he emerges to find out what the Emperor might want with him. The Emperor presents as great a contrast to the meek Pope as could be imagined. A man of commanding confidence, with a bull neck, a German (not Roman) nose, and piercing blue eyes, Constantine has come here to describe his great victory over Maxentius, and the vision of Christ that he believes propelled him to victory. Excitedly, he tells his story.

Miltiades does not know what to make of this story. He is thunderstruck, speechless. Constantine wonders if the little man has lost his tongue? Another man, Silvester, happens to be present to interpret because each is foreign to Latin culture and language. Constantine from Germany. Miltiades from Africa.

Constantine vows to reverse Roman policy toward Christians. He wants to know where the bones of St. Peter are located. Is the cross of Christ in existence? And how about the nails that were used to crucify Jesus? Miltiades tries to answer all these questions truthfully, but he is skeptical, nervous. What does the Emperor want, really?

Constantine explains: He wants to be an apostle for Jesus. He wants to wear one of those nails on his crown. Everywhere he goes, he will fight on behalf of Christ from now on.

To the sixty-two-year-old Miltiades, the thirty-nine-year-old Emperor confides boldly, "In the future, we as the apostle of Christ will help choose the bishop of Rome." Perhaps he was remembering how the Caesars claimed for themselves the right to choose the High Priest at the temple in Jerusalem. Possibly, Miltiades is remembering that that alliance had not turned out too well.

The following day, Constantine returns, full of plans that he has dreamed up in the night. He will build a basilica for Peter here, another for Paul there, to house the bones of these great saints. To quote Malachi Martin:

Miltiades nods, but he is too dazed to answer. The idea of a Christian basilica is too much for him. All his life, he has only known the little churches and chapels, the "dominica" houses of the Lord—really little back rooms. For Miltiades a basilica has always been a pagan building in whose central portion, the apse, there was the Augusteum, a place filled with the statues of the emperors who were worshiped as divinities by the Romans.

...From the Vatican Hill, the party proceeds over to the Lateran Hill. All the palaces and houses here once belonged to the great ancient Roman family of Laterani. Now, one palace, the largest, is the property of Constantine's queen, Fausta—part of her dowry as daughter of the Emperor Maximilian. The ceremony between Constantine and Miltiades here is simple. Constantine throws open the main doors, and states sonorously, "Henceforth, this is the House of Miltiades and of every successor of the blessed apostle, Peter."[20]

Miltiades is not destined to live much longer. He will enjoy his new comforts and status for only fifteen months. At his death, Constantine will appoint Silvester as the new Pope. The assembled Christians of Rome will approve in chorus, grateful to have an emperor who cares about them. Honored, really. They are not used to this sort of favor. No one suspects that they might be establishing a tradition that will cause them centuries of trouble later on.

Sylvester I

Now Silvester is Pope, and he is much more comfortable with his relationship with the Emperor than Miltiades had been. Constantine relates to him more comfortably, too; manages to confess his sins to the Pontiff, and the two are off to a good start being "joint apostles" for Christ, as it were. In conversation, the two men fire each other up with a vision for a truly universal, united Church that conquers the world. They will spread Rome and Roman rule so that "the baptism of Jesus flows on Roman aqueducts to the four quarters of the earth."[21] They decide to make Sunday a public holiday. All local bishops will have civil jurisdiction. Pope Silvester and his successors will have supreme civil jurisdiction over all localities in the western half of the Roman Empire. Malachi Martin concludes:

> ... *This is how Silvester now understands what Jesus said to Peter on that long-distant day near Mount Hermon: "I give to you the keys of the kingdom of Heaven. Whatever you allow on earth will be what Heaven allows. Whatever you forbid on earth will be what Heaven forbids."*
>
> *Still more profound is the effect Silvester's decision (to co-operate with the Emperor) will have on the internal structure of the church. For, under this new conception, that structure will take on all the trappings and manners of political and economic power centered in Rome as a capital. In fact, from this moment on, the spiritual power of Peter is enslaved in the pomp of empire. Far from liberating the church, Silvester's decision has trapped it—even though the cage is studded with jewels and lined with ermine, and the bars are made of gold.*[22]

8

THE DESERT WOMB: ANTONY

Historians, including Church historians, have paid a great deal of attention to these grand events in Rome. Yet often, God does not work through grand events. Sometimes He works silently, often in remote areas of His world and among people in forgotten corners who are just as important and just as loved as are kings and emperors.

The wilderness is God's womb. God sometimes chooses deserts to nurture kingdom movements. Perhaps it is because Egypt has so much desert that it has so often become the womb for God to gestate what He wants to do next. Jacob, that man who became Israel, would go to Egypt, like Abraham before him, and like the family of Jesus after him. In each case, Egypt was a place of hidden gestation, as God prepared the next part of His kingdom plan.

And so, when it came time for the kingdom of God to spread west in the fourth century, once again, the gestation happened in the deserts of Egypt. Who expected this? No one. Who remembers this? Very few.

Spiritual Warfare

In the desert, God has us to Himself. Except that the evil one is there too.

> *Jesus, full of the Holy Spirit, left the Jordan and was led by the Spirit into the wilderness, where for forty days he was tempted by the devil.*

Luke 4:1-2

Many, many of the first Christians followed Jesus into the wilderness, where they too confronted the devil. For them, Christianity was warfare. And they were eager for battle because they had discovered that Christ is the victor.

Such a one was Antony. This illiterate Egyptian was full of zeal, ready for a fight, ready to push back the darkness and establish the kingdom of light by the authority of Jesus. No one in the history of kingdom advance stands quite as tall as Antony. No one had more influence. No one created more transformation for the sake of Jesus than this one man, who became the model for thousands and thousands of kingdom citizens in future.

And yet: today, he is all but forgotten.

Wombs are forgotten places. After the birth happens, people are ready to forget all about wombs. Perhaps this is why Antony has been so completely forgotten. Besides, Antony would be considered strange by today's standards. And that is an understatement. But in his own day, thousands and thousands of people wanted to be like him; his life had such power! And that power had an amazing reach into the future. Centuries into the future!

During the Reformation, twelve hundred years later, reformers would hold up Augustine as a paragon of virtue and right thinking. All well and good. But where did Augustine get his inspiration from? He was more than a great theologian; he was a man of prayer. And his inspiration for prayer and the Christian life was from his fellow African: Antony.

During the Middle Ages, God poured out His Spirit periodically in monastic reform movements. Among the greatest of these was the Cistercian movement of the eleventh and twelfth century, with Bernard of Clairvaux at its center. Where did these monastics get their inspiration from? From Benedict of Nursia and the Rule of St. Benedict six centuries earlier. But where did Benedict get his inspiration? From Cassian and Martin of Tours—who got theirs from the Desert Fathers and Mothers—and from Antony, the very beginning of that desert wellspring. You see how the roads of spiritual renewal all seem to lead back to this one man, for centuries into the future! Maybe we should find out what happened in that desert womb!

The Life of Antony was written up soon after Antony's death by his good friend Athanasius, one of the leading Christians in Alexandria. Athanasius was one of those deeply devoted believers who worried about the increasing worldliness of the Church after 313 AD, and there is little doubt that he wrote up his story of Antony's life as an antidote to an increasingly worldly church. Also: being so close to his subject—knowing Antony so well for so many years—we don't need to worry about whether his stories are accurate. As a historical document, this biography is as good as it gets during this early period.

Antony's Prayer Battle

In his early years, Antony would visit well-known Egyptian Christians he respected, asking them to teach him everything they knew about the way of Jesus. They discipled him in kingdom ways. Then at age thirty-five, he imagined that he was ready to launch out into kingdom warfare.

There was a graveyard in his town that was known as the haunt of demons. Antony had a friend close him in one of the tombs. He was going to challenge the powers of darkness! But the experiment did not turn out as he had expected.

His friend came back the next day, opened the tomb, found Antony lifeless, and carried him back to his family. Returning to consciousness, Antony was full of horror stories of demons overpowering him and beating him up! Yet, he insisted on being taken back to the tomb. He still believed that Jesus Christ would bring a different outcome. There, closed in among the tombs once again, lying on the ground in his weakness, he cried out, "'Here I am—Antony! I do not run from your blows, for even if you give me more, nothing shall separate me from the love of Christ.' Then he also sang, *Though an army should set itself in array against me, my heart shall not be afraid.*"[23]

Demons took the shapes of wild animals, coming at him with violence. Yet Antony kept his confidence in the victory of Jesus. Finally:

> …*The Lord did not forget the wrestling of Antony, but came to his aid. For when he looked up he saw the roof being opened, as it seemed, and a certain beam of light descending toward him. Suddenly the demons vanished from view, the pain of his body ceased instantly, and the building was once more intact. Aware of the assistance and*

both breathing more easily and relieved from the sufferings, Antony entreated the vision that appeared, saying, "Where were you? Why didn't you appear in the beginning, so that you could stop my distresses?" And a voice came to him: "I was here, Antony, but I waited to watch your struggle. And now, since you persevered and were not defeated, I will be your helper forever, and I will make you famous everywhere." On hearing this, he stood up and prayed, and he was so strengthened that he felt that his body contained more might than ever before.[24]

For Athanasius, Antony's life had a message to it, which is why Athanasius went to all the trouble to write about it:

Christians who are sincerely devoted to him (Jesus) and truly believe in him not only prove that the demons, whom the Greeks consider gods, are not gods, but also trample and chase them away as deceivers and corrupters of mankind, through Jesus Christ our Lord, to whom belongs glory forever and ever. Amen.[25]

Antony, through the book of Athanasius, "became famous everywhere," just as Jesus had promised him at age thirty-five. In the next seventy years, that is exactly what happened: he became famous for the rest of his one hundred and five years and for centuries afterward. And it all began with that prayer battle in the graveyard.

Eventually, Antony discipled other Egyptians, thereby multiplying himself. Hundreds of prayer warriors hither and yon received Athanasius' manuscript, *The Life of Antony*, copied it, and sold the copies far and wide, especially to the west. In this way, they earned a living, which kept them in prayer.

Here would be the true seed of the kingdom that grew westward, spread its branches like the "mustard tree," and overwhelmed the demonic forces that had enslaved the Celtic tribes for centuries. To this day, there are Celtic crosses in Scotland and Ireland, preserved these last 1300 years, that have chiseled on their stone crossbeams, scenes from the life of Antony.[26] These crosses prove beyond a shadow of a doubt the international appeal of this one man for generations and for centuries. How could God use an illiterate Egyptian to have such a transformational influence to the ends of the earth?

Antony had come to believe that "the soul's intensity is strong when the pleasures of the body are weakened." He, therefore, adopted an ascetic lifestyle and decided to live alone in the desert. He located an abandoned fortress in the desert, chased out all the snakes and lizards, made the place home, and lived there for the next twenty years. In this way, he learned to listen to God, like John the Baptist. He had learned this: Youthful bravado will get you nowhere. Learn to listen to God.

In future generations, Christian leaders and intercessors would adopt radically different lifestyles from this that Antony chose. Few would be ascetic or live in the desert. But clear away the lifestyle weirdness and asceticism, and you come up with a life devoted to connecting with God. And you come up with the By-My-Spirit lifestyle and its seven ingredients.

At the end of the twenty years, some townspeople discovered him and tore down his door. He emerged from his self-imposed exile. And then: "Through him, the Lord healed many of those present who suffered from bodily ailments; others he purged of demons, and to Antony he gave grace of speech…. (H)e persuaded many to take up the solitary life. And so, from then on, there were monasteries in the mountains, and the desert was made a city by monks, who left their own people and registered themselves for the citizenship in the heavens."[27]

This is the official beginning of the monastic movement in the West. It shows very clearly that the kingdom of God did not originally lean on the worldly power of Empire but put its confidence in prayer and the Holy Spirit.

Perhaps a little further explanation would help. The word "monk" comes from the word "mono," which means "one." Originally, the movement consisted of people using the desert as a prayer closet, in response to the words of Jesus, "But when you pray, go into your room, close the door and pray to your Father, who is unseen. Then your Father, who sees what is done in secret, will reward you" (Matthew 6:6). Antony lived alone. Therefore, the goal of the first monasteries was to imitate Antony, even though there would be some measure of community, and they would encourage each other and disciple new arrivals. But the word *monastery* reflects this solitary lifestyle in the desert that started with Antony.

Humility Producing Discipleship

Antony was reluctant to allow anyone to consider him a great saint, even when he received inquiries from emperors. This tendency to idolize him (and future Christian "saints") prevented people from learning how to walk in kingdom authority for themselves, as illustrated by the following story:

> ...A certain military officer named Martinianus became a nuisance to Antony. He had a daughter who was disturbed by a demon, so that he stayed a long while, rapping on the

door and asking him to come out and to pray to God on his daughter's behalf. He was unwilling to open the door but stooping from above said, "Why do you cry out to me, man? I too am a man like you, but if you believe in Christ, whom I serve, go, and in the same way you believe, pray to God, and it will come to pass." Immediately he departed, believing and calling on Christ and having his daughter purified of the demon.... Through Antony, many other things have been done by the Lord, who says, Ask, and it will be given you. For though he did not open the door, great numbers of those who suffered simply spent nights outside his cell, and were cleansed when they believed and prayed with sincerity.[28]

This little story shows how Antony wanted people to become disciples of Jesus and citizens of a new kingdom. He wanted them to learn how to walk in the power and anointing of the Holy Spirit for themselves. It models out for us the connection between a kingdom lifestyle and the Great Commission of the Church—to make disciples, "teaching people to obey what I have commanded." Again, the Church prospered not as a religious institution doing Sunday services but as a network of discipleship communities. Disciple-makers shied away from hero-worship.

Fathering a Movement

Eventually, Antony was so beset with crowds of people that he decided to move to a more isolated region of desert in the south of Egypt, the mountainous upper Thebaid. Here he planted a garden and made a self-sufficient existence while maintaining the life of prayer and complete solitude.

Not exactly the lifestyle you would expect of a man who is to "become famous everywhere."

But the hermit lifestyle had been spreading throughout Egypt with a life all its own, and these young prayer warriors searched Antony out in his new mountain retreat for teaching and training in how to conduct themselves. As he taught them, we have the very first hints of a monastic rule, which is nothing but Antony's way of making disciples.

> For all the monks who came to him he unfailingly had the same message: to have faith in the Lord and love him; to guard themselves from lewd thoughts and pleasures of the flesh, and as it is written in Proverbs, not to be deceived by the feeding of the belly; to flee vanity, and to pray constantly; to sing holy songs before sleep and after, and to take to heart the precepts in the Scriptures; to keep in mind the deeds of the saints, so that the soul, ever mindful of the commandments, might be educated by their ardor. But he especially urged them to practice constantly the word of the Apostle, Do not let the sun go down on your anger, and to consider that this had been spoken with every commandment in mind—so that the sun should set neither on anger nor on any other sin of ours.[29]

In his distant house of prayer, God would sometimes reveal to Antony people that were on their way to visit him, sometimes two or three months in advance, and the reason why they were coming to visit him. At other times, God would show Antony crises that were happening in other places so that he could pray for those who were involved. At other times, people would experience Antony's prayers for people in crisis back home, and, upon returning home, they will have been healed at the precise moment of Antony's distant prayer.

The Big City

At one point toward the end of his life, Antony was encouraged to visit the great city of Alexandria.

> *Both Greeks and those among them who are called priests came to the Lord's house, saying, "We ask to see the man of God"—for this is what everyone called him. And there also the Lord cleansed many people of demons through him, and cured those who were mentally impaired. Many Greeks asked only to touch the old man, believing they would be benefited. It is beyond doubt that as many became Christians in those few days as one would have seen in a year.*[30]

The visit to Alexandria attracted a completely different class of people into Antony's circle of acquaintances—the Greek philosophers and intellectuals. And they found themselves content to be lectured by an illiterate sage, who said:

> *Tell us, then, where are your oracles now? Where are the incantations of the Egyptians? Where are the magicians' phantasms? When, except at the time the cross of Christ came, did all these things come to an end and lost their strength? Is it this cross, then, that is worthy of ridicule—or the things, instead, that have been nullified and proved weak by it? For this too is a wonder: Your religion was never persecuted, and in every city, it is honored among men, and yet our doctrines flourish and increase beyond yours. Your views perish, though acclaimed and celebrated far and*

wide. But the faith and teaching of Christ, ridiculed by you and persecuted frequently by rulers, has filled the world."[31]

The remainder of this book tells the story of how God used this one man to transform nations all the way to Ireland. But a storyteller can sense when his audience is getting uneasy. I know what you are thinking: "But Antony was so weird. A diet of bread and water for months at a time? A total recluse living in the desert? Are you kidding? Is this what you have to do to advance the kingdom of God? Seriously?"

So let me put it this way. This ascetic lifestyle was indeed Antony's trademark. By this, we can trace his influence. To this day, there exist hermits' prayer huts preserved on remote Irish islands in the Atlantic Ocean from the sixth century, testimony to Antony's influence for centuries to come, all the way to Ireland. To the west, thousands would look at Antony and say, "I want to be like that." And they did.

But it was not his severe lifestyle that attracted them. It was the authority and the power that emanated from him. He was a kingdom man—a whole new concept for people to come to grips with. Many assumed that his ascetic lifestyle was what produced his power.

But as I trace the story of the next generations, you will notice that they will soon come to re-evaluate this assumption. Eventually, they will discover that asceticism was not, of itself, a necessary part of the kingdom lifestyle. A sifting would take place, as I will show. And what will emerge is the seven-part lifestyle that I am calling "By-My-Spirit" Christianity.

9

ALL FALL DOWN

Now let's go back to Rome to see what is happening with Silvester's more matronly come-of-age Church, which has incorporated an emperor's plans into its destiny. Silvester is about to be visited by a very important group of people—the descendants of the family of Jesus from Jerusalem. To understand the importance of this visit, we have to go back to Rome's relations with the Jews over the last three centuries.

When Rome destroyed Jerusalem, they didn't just tear down the temple Herod had built (as Yeshua had prophesied). They demolished the city itself, the walls, the houses, the shops. Everything! Flat on the ground! All turned into rubble. An almost supernatural fury. The only structures they left standing were the three towers of Herod's Palace because it had been the residence of the Roman governor. The Romans wanted to remind the Jews about the power of Rome. Let Jewish people never forget the power of Rome! (Of course, the foundation stones of the Temple Mount, today called "The Western Wall," below ground level, remained in place.)

Early in the second century, following the Bar Kokhba revolt, Emperor Hadrian added insult to injury by forbidding Jews to live in Jerusalem at all, and he changed the name of Judea to Syria Palaestia as if to erase the whole idea of Jewishness.

Sylvester and the Descendants of Jesus

The contempt of Rome toward Jews (who had been allowed to return to Jerusalem by then) surfaced again in 318 when the descendants of the family of Jesus visited Pope Sylvester, newly ensconced in his palace in Rome. Since the time of Hadrian, Greek-speaking leaders had displaced the original Jewish leaders of the Church in Jerusalem. The descendants of Jesus and the first apostles had been edged out of their positions of leadership. And so, five years after the Edict of Milan, here came the *desposyni*, the direct descendants of the family of Jesus to Pope Sylvester in Rome, making two requests.[32] First, they asked Sylvester to honor them by restoring them as leaders of the Church at Jerusalem. Second, they asked for a cash donation (similar to the one the apostle Paul had collected as recorded in 2 Corinthians 8) out of compassion but also out of respect for the Church of Jerusalem as the mother church of Christianity. Malachi Martin describes the Pope's response:

> *Sylvester curtly and decisively dismissed the claims of the Jewish Christians. He told them that the mother church was now in Rome, with the bones of the Apostle Peter, and he insisted that they accept Greek bishops to lead them.*
>
> *It was the last known discussion between the Jewish Christians of the old mother church and the non-Jewish Christians of the new mother church.[33]*

Shortly after this disastrous interview, all traces of a Messianic Jewish presence disappeared.

The apostle Paul had built a bridge between Jews and Gentiles in order to communicate the Gospel from its Jewish source to its Gentile destination. Silvester burned the bridge to the ground.

To Silvester and his Emperor, it looked like they had an unbeatable combination. God had thrown away the Jews, apparently. Now Rome was to be the Eternal City, which would become the new venue for the One True Religion. The Empire would provide the military cover, while the Popes would be given responsibilities over the ordering of society. This was how they conceived the kingdom of God now, and this version of the kingdom of God spread out to the west. The disciple-making community of Jesus was converted into a religious institution in league with the Emperor of Rome.

The "One True Religion" in Britain

And so it was that, during the fourth century, following the Edict of Milan, Rome planted churches that conducted Mass on Sunday mornings in Britain among the Celts. There was a bishopric in London, another at Lincoln, and another at York. So, yes, to that extent, the Roman Church did spread Christianity into Britain during the fourth century.

But has there ever been a case in the history of the world where one country occupied another country by military might, and the occupied people thanked God for the privilege of being occupied? Rome required a third of their army to be stationed among the Celts in order to keep them "civilized." They had attempted to push their control north to Carlisle. And for a brief time, they had even built a wall, the Antonine Wall, between Dumbarton and Sterling in the far north. But the region known as Strathclyde had proved too unstable, too hostile, and so they had to retreat back to Hadrian's Wall, located a little south of today's Scottish Border with England, south of the Firth of Solway. So it was the people south of this wall who were to gain the benefits of Roman Christianity. Not the crusty Northerners who occupied Scotland of today.

By the end of the fourth century, though, everyone knew that the whole Empire was in deep trouble. Within eighty years of Silvester's alliance with Constantine, it began to look like the Church was chained to a dead body, trying to drag itself through the forests. The barbarians of Europe, it seemed, did not prefer Roman "civilization" and were invading the Empire from the north.

In a desperate attempt to provide stability, a general with a Welsh mother and a Welsh wife made his move in 406 to gain control of the situation. Put forward by the Roman army, who felt the need for a strong hand, he called himself Constantine the Third, Emperor of the Western Roman Empire. Constantine III lasted four years as co-Emperor with Honorius. After that, overwhelmed by chaos, he abdicated.

Then he was murdered.

Then God Arose

Then, in 411, the whole structure of the Roman Empire among the Celts collapsed, including the churches. Robert Van de Weyer described the catastrophe in his book, *Celtic Fire:*

...Christianity never took root in Roman Britain. The great majority of Christians were either Roman colonists or Britons that had adopted Roman attitudes and customs, while to the Celtic tribesmen, Christianity was despised as the religion of oppression, no better than the older Roman cults in which the emperor was held up for worship. Thus when the Roman Empire fell early in the fifth century, and Angles and Saxons swept across the south and east of the country, Christianity virtually disappeared. Only a handful of British Christians escaped into the hills of Wales, where they practiced their religion in secret.

Yet by the early decades of the fifth century, a new Christian mission was enjoying astonishing success, penetrating those areas of Celtic Britain which had never fallen to Roman conquest. This time it was not grand governors riding in elegant chariots who carried the gospel, but barefoot monks plodding the muddy lanes.[34]

God had not decreed that the Roman Church would link arms with the Emperor, and the two would march west together in wonderful triumph, helping each other to conquer the world. As much as this had seemed like a good plan, this version of Power-and-Might Christianity was not God's intent.

This is what God had decreed:

In the time of those kings, the God of heaven will set up a kingdom that will never be destroyed, nor will it be left to another people. It will crush all those kingdoms and bring them to an end, but it will itself endure forever.

Daniel 2:44

For some reason, historians have been reluctant to own up to the utter failure of Constantine's religious experiment in Britain. The idea that Britain gained its Christian faith from Rome has stuck like Gorilla Glue to Church history books and Hollywood movies. But more and more students of history have to admit, with Robert van de Weyer, what should have been apparent all along: Power-And-Might Christianity was a failure. Let us get this clear at last. Power-and-Might Christianity is always a failure. Rome simply did not know how to win the hearts of the Celtic people to the Lord Jesus Christ. And its idea of the kingdom of God had become twisted beyond recognition. What Rome said was the kingdom of God was not the kingdom of God.

But God had made His decree. And God is faithful to do what He says He will do. His methods, His love, His kindness are all infinitely higher than ours. He had a different plan than Constantine and Silvester had hatched eighty years before. And it was exactly what God had prophesied in Daniel 2. The kingdom of God was planted in the rubble of a collapsing Fourth Empire, but the way it was planted was "By-My-Spirit," not "Power-and-Might."

In 410, Alaric, King of the Visigoths, invaded Rome with an army of Goths whose wives and children had just been wantonly murdered in a great bloodbath by Emperor Honorius. Fueled by revenge for this gross barbarity, the Gothic army destroyed Rome. The city went up in flames, much worse than in Nero's time. Great villas were cast down to the ground. Also in flames were the neat plans of emperors and popes for an alliance that would win the world for Christ.

But in 397, God started something new in Celt country, and it went all the way to the farthest shores of Ireland. As the Roman churches collapsed to the south (today's England), a garden of love was being planted like seeds in the cold ground of the north, where you might have thought that the ground was too cold to sustain a garden. But in the deserts of Egypt, the seedlings had already sprouted in the seed trays. And even now, God was bringing the trays out of the greenhouse to get them ready for transplanting into Celt country.

10

THE EVAGRIUS GENERATION

Someone had to take the lifestyle of the Desert and communicate it outward so that you wouldn't have to go to the desert and become a monk to learn it. That person was Evagrius of Pontus.

As a young man, Evagrius had become Archdeacon in the Eastern Church under Gregory Nazianzus. Very quickly, the Church in Constantinople was betraying the fascination for external glory and pomp that was also overtaking the Church at Rome. Evagrius found this intoxicating.

One day, he met a beautiful woman who fell deeply in love with him. He could not resist her; she could not resist him. But the problem was: she was married to a prosperous merchant in the great city. And with each clandestine rendezvous, Evagrius' conscience troubled him more and more. One day, according to a mini-biography by a contemporary named Palladius, Evagrius had a dream.

> ... *There appeared to him an angel vision in the shape of soldiers of the governor, and they seized him and took him apparently to the tribunal and threw him into the so-called custody, the men who had come to him, as it seemed, without giving a reason having first fastened his neck and hands with iron collars and chains. But he knew in his conscience*

that for the sake of the above fault, he was suffering these things and imagined that her husband had intervened.[35]

After much anxiety, when all seemed lost, the angel of the Lord said to him (in the dream): "It is not expedient for you to stay in this city…Swear to me that you will leave this city and care for your soul, and I will free you…." Evagrius promised the angel that he would leave Constantinople—and his high position in the Church. Immediately, he loaded up as many of his belongings as he could take with him on a ship bound for Jerusalem. He was going to learn how to care for his soul in the city where it all began, the city of rubble.

He soon arrived in the ruined Holy City. There, he came in contact with a woman who had already become a leader in the prayer movement in the desert: Melania, today known as Melania the Younger.

This woman is larger than life, and when you read her story, you wonder if such a person could have existed. But there are two ancient biographies of her, and present-day archeologists have located her estate on the Coelian Hill in Rome. This estate burned to the ground when Alaric sacked Rome in 410 AD. But she was no longer there. She was in the desert, becoming a leader of the prayer movement.

Melania the Younger

Born in 383 AD, Melania had grown up in, surely, the wealthiest family in Rome. Her grandfather had been Prefect of Rome. As a young girl, she inherited vast wealth, including the estate in Rome, a villa on the coast of Italy, another villa in Sicily, and properties in Spain, Africa, Mauretania, Britain, Numidia, Aquitania, and Gaul. Her estate in Thagaste, Africa, was larger than the city itself. She owned thousands and thousands of slaves.[36] The only way I can explain what happened to her is this, that God required someone to fund the prayer movement and chose her for the purpose. How else, to explain this:

Married at the age of fourteen, she and her young husband, Pinian, came under the influence of the prayer movement that was raging in Egypt. Immediately, the two of them began to convert their vast holdings into cash, to support the poor, to build hospitals, and, above all, to build houses of prayer. We wish we had a personal story to explain this amazing realization about the futility of wealth, so rare in every age. The two of them moved to Africa, where they were befriended by Augustine of Hippo. Augustine's circle of friends had been deeply influenced by reading *The Life of Antony*.

The young couple then traveled to Alexandria, visited the monks of Nitria for several months, then settled in Jerusalem, where Melania founded a house of prayer for women at the Mount of Olives. It must have been quite early in this part of her life that Evagrius showed up while she was still converting her holdings into cash and funding houses of prayer and ministries to the poor and the sick. Eventually, all her wealth was given away. All of it! Somewhere about this time, her husband died, but she went on to become one of the great leaders of prayer in her time, based in Jerusalem near or on the Mount of Olives.

Evagrius Meets Melania

Evagrius showed up in the city of rubble, still flaunting his position as a churchman, prancing around in his impressive clothes. But one day, he became deathly ill and almost died. Melania visited him after six months of this sickness, and she had a serious conversation with him. He told her all about the dream he had had in Constantinople, the angel, and how he had been challenged to "guard his soul." He realized that God was dealing with him, allowing him to come very close to death, and Melania agreed. So she challenged him to go to Nitria and learn from the disciples of Antony how to "guard his soul." Then she prayed for him—and immediately, his condition began to improve. In three days, he was completely restored—and he did as she had instructed. He moved to Nitria.

Picture it. He shows up in this small-town community of illiterate monks, most of whom don't speak Greek, only a local Egyptian dialect. They are suspicious of foreigners and are not impressed with his learning, his high position in Constantinople, or his impressive clothes. But he humbles himself before them and asks them to teach him all they know about how to guard one's soul. They take him on and begin to disciple this Archdeacon of the high Church in the Big City. They may have taught him Origen's method of opening his spirit to the Holy Spirit breathing upon the scriptures, a method which would later be known as *Lectio Divina*, or "Divine Reading."[37] He stayed with them for two years, learning the ways of the Desert. They taught him how to be an ascetic, and he went on a more or less permanent diet of bread and water. Then he left the discipling community, renounced the world, and became a true hermit in the desert at Cellia.

It is largely because of Evagrius that we know what the early Desert Fathers believed and practiced. He was the first to write it down and publish books about it. (I recommend *Praktikos and Chapters on Prayer*, two writings that have been published as one volume by the Cistercians.)

Let me summarize the writings of Evagrius to showcase the importance of this man in advancing the kingdom of God. This is the By-My-Spirit culture that was growing up in the Deserts of Egypt:

They said if you want to be an effective Christian, you have to learn four skills, and they are all prayer skills. In other words, Christianity is about the unique authority of prayer that God has given us through the death of Jesus on the Cross.

Four Principles of the Desert

First, we learn to connect with God daily. We have to develop a consistent relationship with Him. Daily. Not on Sundays only. Or on Christmas and Easter.

Second, we learn to let His love flow into us. We become anchored in His love, for "while we were yet sinners, Christ died for the ungodly." It is not about trying to be good people. It's about allowing God's heart of love to affect our hearts. Daily. We expose ourselves to His unconditional love. We let Him smile on us, and we absorb His thoughts.

Third, we learn that the evil one tries to keep us from doing steps one and two. Therefore, we have to discern these methods of resistance and stage a resistance of our own. "Resist the devil and he will flee from you. Draw near to God and he will draw near to you" (James 4:7-8). There is an inner battle that we must become aware of against distractions and against deadly thought patterns, which lead to spiritual death (see below). The Desert Fathers became experts at discerning how to wage this interior warfare in order to consistently draw near to God.

The apostle John had written the prophetic words of Jesus in the book of Revelation, chapters 2 and 3: "To those who overcome, I will give…." There follow in John's writing many wonderful gifts that Jesus gives to overcomers. In the desert, they were learning how to be overcomers and how to receive those gifts from the King. But they are received in the midst of spiritual conflict. They don't glide easily into a person's life like Christmas gifts from Santa Claus.

Fourth, we learn how to aggressively defeat the works of demons in the world around us by discerning the difference between God's goodness and the subtle counterfeits of the evil one, who sometimes masquerades as an angel of light (2 Corinthians 11:14). We become suited for this warfare by becoming skilled at step one and step two. The closer we remain to the heart of God, the more discerning we become. Then by prayer and prayer ministry, we push back the darkness around us, bringing the unconditional love of God into our communities. Ministering to the poor. Freeing slaves. Getting rid of sin industries. Casting out demons. Doing what Jesus did.

The Desert Fathers and Mothers were full of the gifts of the Spirit for ministry. They routinely ministered deliverance, healing, words of knowledge, prophecy, and miracles. But the gift that was prized most highly among them was the word of wisdom. True wisdom was attained only by those who were practiced in resisting the devil and drawing near to God—and had been doing it for years.

Evagrius was best known for cataloging the "eight deadly thoughts" that lead us away from God into spiritual cul-de-sacs and addictions. Two centuries later, Gregory the Great would convert these into the "seven deadly sins." But Evagrius reminds us that the true struggle begins in the thought life, the interior of our hearts. It is not about trying to avoid sin patterns but taking time to draw near to God. The enemy does not want us drawing near to God, and he fights us all the way on the journey "through the curtain" into the Holy of Holies, which is now located in all the nations.

My Encounter with Evagrius

My first encounter with Evagrius was in the teaching of Diogenes Allen of Princeton, who introduced him to a group of us pastors and elaborated on "the eight deadly thoughts." I was going through a deep spiritual struggle at the time, the result of a prayer battle, and I knew I needed some answers from outside of American culture. I needed some handles to understand what was happening to me, and Diogenes Allen's presentation of Evagrius' writings was just the ticket. In his book, *Spiritual Theology: The Theology of Yesterday for Spiritual Help Today,* [38] Dr. Allen presents the blindness that most of us suffer from, who have grown up in the West:

The Christian vocabulary of self-renunciation, rejection of pride, and obedience violently clashes with contemporary culture, which values self-affirmation, self-realization, self-esteem, and empowerment. It is certainly correct for us to turn away from self-rejection, which is a very powerful tendency within us, but to understand the Christian language of self-renunciation, we need to understand the role of social prestige in the way we evaluate ourselves and our worth. Although we want to think well of ourselves, we cannot love ourselves directly, and this leads us to desire, admire, seek or love what has social prestige and value and to identify ourselves with it. Then we can think well of ourselves. We are proud to be members of an excellent football team or a respected profession, or to work for a major company. We bask in the reflected glory of something society esteems, and it gives us self-esteem and energy.

According to Christian teachings, if our self-understanding and self-evaluation arise wholly from our social position, then we cannot receive them from God. Whether we have a high or low self-evaluation, we cannot perceive the potential God has in store for us. That is why God's call to liberation, to freedom from this distorted view of ourselves, is heard as a call to self-destruction. The call to reject pride, to become humble and to make sacrifices sounds oppressive, beside the point, and clearly not the way to live happily.[39]

Desert wisdom would have us turning up our noses at lesser things in order to go after the higher things. Evagrius had already discovered the shallowness of basing his life on social position and the esteem of other people, including Church people. He went to the desert to find the ultimate identity that could be found only in God, as a citizen of the kingdom of God. This is the deep insight of the Desert Mothers and Fathers. To find security in the opinions and outward splendor of social institutions, even in the Church, is a slippery slope with no solid ground to stand on. Jesus alone is a solid Rock.

But to get to the Rock, we have to deal with the false identities society recommends to us, including the Church. Westerners say: "Here, devote yourself to this, and if you succeed, you can believe in yourself, your worth, the significance of your life." But once Evagrius attained the Desert, he had to turn against thought patterns that society had taught him to rely on, which were unreliable. These are the "eight deadly thoughts" which he articulated in his writings. And they are just as deadly today as they were in the fourth century. These all lead us into dead-ends that are short of God. And these are virtually an exact description of life in America and in most Western cultures today.

The "Hallway with Nine Doors"

There is not enough space here to thoroughly describe these deadly patterns of thought; I recommend Diogenes Allen's book for this. But if we want to understand the culture that brought the West to Christ, we have to get inside the heads and hearts of the Desert Fathers and Mothers because they, far more than Rome, were the ones who transformed the world in the early days. Let me simply list each of the "deadly thoughts" in brief:

1. First, Evagrius describes the temptation to live for food, for physical enjoyments and pleasures, which short-circuit receiving and giving love, the true purpose of life.

2. Second, he describes the lust for sexual pleasure, which can become such a great and controlling desire that it overwhelms all genuine love.

3. The third deadly thought is avarice, the desire to seek security for the future, and worldly position in the present, through accumulating possessions. We become so busy managing possessions, we have no time left for God or for kingdom love.

4. The next deadly thought, sadness, arises when we compare our achievements with those of others and find we are deeply disappointed with our lives.

5. The passion of anger, like sadness, is concerned with our relationships with other people who have hurt us or failed to properly appreciate and respect us. We end up wallowing in offense.

6. The final three deadly thoughts have to do with our intentions to make progress in the Christian life. Dr. Allen writes: "At first we may be so pleased at having achieved some order and direction in our fragmented and disordered lives that we cannot imagine wanting anything beyond that— but in time we may be afflicted with *accidia,* traditionally called 'sloth' but better understood as boredom or apathy that leads to despair....Despair arises from discouragement over our lack of personal progress in the Christian life, the failures of fellow Christians, mean-spiritedness, and gossip, and church politics. Love between Christians is not in evidence; no one seems genuinely interested in anyone else. In short, despair is what tells us that we do not seem to be getting anywhere...."[40]

7. Vainglory is just the opposite reaction. As we sense we are making progress in our life with God, we want everyone to notice our progress. We try to fill other peoples' minds with ourselves.

8. Frequently, vainglory is accompanied by pride, the eighth deadly thought. Pride causes us to take full credit for the progress we have made. This leads to a sense of superiority. And pride goes before a fall.

All of these teachings about deadly thoughts were developed in the context of communities of people who were actively going after God. Take them out of that context, and they become mere legalisms. Picture them as doors in a hallway, where the final door is the love of God. If we can just make it to the final door, past the eight side entries, all of which lead to cul-de-sacs, we can anchor ourselves in the love of God, the only true source of peace and significance.

The kingdom of God is the discovery of that love, where it becomes real, it feeds you, it guides you, it protects you day after day. The two central realities, as taught in the Desert, are thus the authority of Christian prayer and the privilege of connecting daily with the love of God despite satanic interference. This was the teaching of the kingdom of God that was growing up in the Desert, and it was this teaching that would flow west to the ends of the earth—all the way to Ireland.

11

MARTIN OF TOURS

Just as Evagrius was moving from Constantinople to the deserts of Egypt, a Hungarian-born Roman soldier named Martin was moving west into Gaul. His father had been a Roman soldier, a tribune, and it was only natural that the son would follow in his father's footsteps. It seems he became a part of the elite bodyguard of the Emperor, and he, therefore, would have seen the Emperor Constans at close quarters. But early in his life, he became a Christian—and Christianity was still a minority religion despite all of Constantine's efforts to make it "official." It would not become truly official until the end of the century, under Theodosius I. When Julian the Apostate succeeded Constans as Emperor, Martin discovered that the old days of hostility toward Christians were not quite over.

So before long, Martin clung to his faith by letting go of the army. He said, "I am a soldier of Christ; it is not lawful for me to fight."[41] He quickly joined himself to the greatest Christian leader in Gaul, Hilary of Poitiers. It must have been at this time that he read *The Life of Antony*, and it changed him forever.[42] He immediately became a hermit, living on an island in the Ligurian sea, on the coast of the Mediterranean facing toward the deserts of Africa.

Martin is the most important link between the deserts of Egypt and the British Isles. He never went to Egypt, but Egypt came to him in the book by Athanasius. We can imagine him saying, "I want to be like Antony; I want to have that kind of authority." Spiritual warfare was a big part of the vision of the Desert Fathers, and many of the leaders of the Celtic Church would start life fighting in one army or another as military men.

Martin spent ten years simply being a hermit, as Antony had been. In addition to prayer, he would minister to the poor in the power of the Holy Spirit so that he became quite well known for the love that radiated from him. He then established a monastery at Ligugé, which was to become the oldest monastery in France (eventually Benedictine, but Benedict had not been born yet).

One day, he was invited to go to Tours, and while he was there, the Christians all got together and elected him to be their bishop. He knew nothing about being a bishop and didn't really want to be one. But in accepting the position, he was ordained while sitting on a milking stool—a statement of opposition to the pretensions of the Roman Church.

As a bishop, he mostly kept doing what he had learned so far. He started what was to become the most influential house of prayer in the history of Europe: Marmoutier, "The Place of the Big Family," just across from the city of Tours along the Loire River. Those he trained then went and built other houses of prayer elsewhere so that quite a prayer movement resulted from the spiritual vibrancy that radiated from Marmoutier.

Marmoutier

This vibrant community demonstrates that what had started out as a hermit movement was turning into a movement of prayer communities. Many would call them monasteries, but Marmoutier was nothing like what we have all come to mean by that term today, so I prefer to call these communities houses of prayer. These were groups of disciples learning how to connect with God and with each other in love, quite similar to the description of the New Testament discipleship community described in Acts 2.

> *They devoted themselves to the apostles' teaching, and to fellowship, to the breaking of bread and to prayer. Everyone was filled with awe at the wonders and signs performed by the apostles. All the believers were together and had everything in common.*

> *Acts 2:42–44*

Martin himself lived in a hut called *Candida Casa*, "The White House" or "Shining Hut."

The life in this community was described by Sulpicius Severus:

> *Many also of the brethren had, in the same manner, fashioned retreats for themselves, but most of them had formed these out of the rock of the overhanging mountain, hollowed into caves. There were altogether eighty disciples, who were being disciplined after the example of the saintly master. No one there had anything which was called his own; all things were possessed in common. It was not allowed either to buy or to sell anything.... No art was practiced there, except that of transcribers, and even this*

was assigned to the brethren of younger years, while the elders spent their time in prayer. Rarely did any one of them go beyond the cell, unless when they assembled at the place of prayer. They all took their food together, after the hour of fasting was past. No one used wine, except when illness compelled them to do so. Most of them were clothed in garments of camels' hair. Any dress approaching to softness was there deemed criminal, and this must be thought the more remarkable, because many among them were such as are deemed of noble rank.[43]

The description here is as opposite from what was happening in Rome as one could imagine. Athanasius had written *The Life of Antony* because he was deeply concerned about what he saw as creeping worldliness in the Church as soon as it became popular to be a Christian. In a way, *The Life of Antony* was a book of protest against what was happening in Rome. It may seem like an extreme antidote, but this antidote proved to be surprisingly popular. Why? I believe it was because God was bestowing a hunger for Himself. I can explain it in no other way. People—even the nobility—were getting sick of what Rome had become. Now an alternative was offering itself, and they were willing to go after it, no matter the cost.

12

NINIAN'S CAVE

One of the novices who came to Marmoutier to be trained was a Briton named Ninian. Ninian then became a missionary to what is today called Scotland. The details of Ninian's life are sketchy; the bits and snatches of biography we have just don't fit together very well. One thing that is known about him is that he lived in a cave as a hermit when he first moved back to Britain from Tours in 397 AD. It was as though a piece of Marmoutier (and the Desert) had transferred itself to the far north.

Ninian's Cave is located on the north shore of the Firth of Solway, which divides present-day England from Scotland. It is just north of Hadrian's Wall, the Roman barrier which separated the "barbarian" North from the "civilized" South.

Ninian's Cave is, to this day, a place of pilgrimage for Scots. When my wife and I went there in 2003, there was a Scottish bagpiper and his son walking the path ahead of us down to the cave. The entire time we were there, he was playing tunes on his bagpipes, pacing back and forth at the mouth of the cave. I have shivers just thinking about it, even today. The cave is a pilgrim destination because this is where Christianity first took root in Scotland.

And Ninian had no idea of the importance of his ministry and the number of people who would be transformed by it. He was just being obedient.

But why would a man sail to the Firth of Solway from the thriving city of Tours to live in a cave all by himself? That is the question. It is said that Ninian came from Strathclyde in the first place, and so he was just returning home. But wouldn't he have lived with his family if that were the case? Why live in a cave? There are many lingering mysteries surrounding Ninian!

My take is this. I believe God did it. I believe that, at one point, as Martin's life was drawing to a close at Tours, God told Ninian that, like many others who were starting houses of prayer, Ninian was to start one too, north of Hadrian's Wall! Ninian was being given a kingdom challenge! It was purely God's decision; that is what I think.

At a recent conference I attended, Thai Lamm said, "Let your life be such that it looks totally foolish unless God is real." This move that Ninian made looks totally foolish—unless God is real. It is a good example of someone who is walking by faith—like Abraham, who set out on a journey and didn't know where he was going. Ninian was a son of Abraham!

Seed of the Celtic Church

Strathclyde, the area of southwest Scotland today, was Welsh and Pictish.[44] Ninian's Cave, located in Strathclyde, is not just the beginning of Christianity in Scotland. It marks the start of the great Celtic awakening in Britain, which became the ancient Celtic Church, spreading from that cave in all directions.

This insight may be new to some, so let me take you to the big picture for a moment to address this idea more broadly. As we look into the future, we will see a unique role for Scotland.

It will be a place where God will plant new seeds of spiritual awakening, let them grow a bit, then send them out to transform other places. These "times of refreshing from the presence of the Lord" will become profoundly abundant in Scotland in future centuries. My friend, Tom Lennie, an Orkney man who has written extensively about the phenomenon of Scottish Revival movements, has tracked in intimate detail how Scotland has been a "land of many revivals," which is the title of one of his three highly researched books[45] about spiritual awakenings in Scotland over the last 450 years.

I maintain that Scotland has had a unique place in the plan of God for longer than 500 years as a greenhouse for revival movements. But, like Egypt, most people are not aware of the unique role that this nation has had as a womb of new spiritual awakenings. The womb, after all, is a hidden place. Whether it's the Presbyterian movement of the 16th century (that showed how God could spiritually awaken nations–see Volume Two), or the role of Presbyterians in the American Great Awakening, Second Great Awakening and the Prayer Revival of 1858, or the role of Presbyterians in the Great Korean Awakening of 1907, or in the Kassia Hills of India in 1906, few are aware of the importance of Scotland in giving birth to spiritual awakenings that matured and prospered elsewhere, outside of Scotland. I believe that role began right here at Ninian's Cave in the year 397: the forgotten beginnings of a hermit, discipled in Tours, then transplanted to Scotland to pray kingdom prayers, relying on God alone and radiating the loving authority of Christ. And all this, before any country called "Scotland" even existed.

What Ninian started here would spread to Ireland, south to present-day Wales, and north to the Picts—slowly warming whole tribes and nations with love. Then, at the proper time, it would return to Scotland at Iona, and then, at last, the Anglo Saxons would receive it into Northumbria and to the country we now call England.

But it all started in Scotland.

At Ninian's cave.

Ninian's Ministry

At one point, Ninian managed to build a house for himself, which became a house of prayer, which he called *Candida Casa*, "The White House" or "Shining Hut" in imitation of Martin. Since Martin had just died, perhaps it was "in memoriam," in honor of Ninian's deceased mentor.

His life in these early years was not an easy one, as we learn from this story Ray Simpson tells:

> *Ninian's pioneer mission in Galloway toward the end of the fourth century was bitterly opposed by the local king, until he was struck by a disease that cost him his sight. The king asked Ninian to forgive him. Following Christ's example, Ninian not only forgave him, but restored his sight. Thus the royal doors became opened to the gospel in northwest Britain.*[46]

Whithorn

Eventually, a full-fledged Christian community sprang up, the first Celtic prayer community in Britain. The community of Whithorn, like Marmoutier, would become a model and inspiration for hundreds, if not thousands of prayer communities throughout Celt country. Ray Simpson, who must surely be the leading authority on the ancient Celtic Church today, [47] concludes: "Ninian's center remained a model of fellowship for countless groupings of monks, nuns, and hermits throughout the Celtic lands."[48]

As all this was happening in the far north, the Roman Empire came crashing down, humbled by the collapse of the very power and might in which the Roman Church had put its confidence.

Christianity was made the official religion of the Roman Empire in 386, although the organized Church in the cities tended to reflect rather than reform society. In 410, when the Goths sacked Rome, Jerome cried out: "O weep for the Empire! Suddenly comes news of Rome's fall. The light of all the earth is extinguished." Rome's fall had been made possible by the debauchery and corruption that had run rampant through the cities of the Empire. Yet, in the darkness of collapse, Jerome sent out news of the beacon fires for Christ that remained alight in the deserts. Living at Bethlehem, Jerome helped keep the flame of holiness burning in the Christians of Gaul by giving them constant news of the lives of the monks in the desert caves of the Thebaid and of Nitria, through his courier Sysinus.[49]

Humbled, the Roman Church would have to discover the inner life of the kingdom of God and learn to sense the leadings of the Spirit of God. Eventually, Benedict of Nursia would draw from the wisdom of the Desert and Martin of Tours to formulate his Rule of St. Benedict.

In the meantime, the Celts were free to follow the leadings of the Holy Spirit, which they learned to call "the wild goose." For like the wild goose in its guided meanderings, the Celts would become skilled at letting an inner voice speak to them, as Ninian had learned to do, obeying the purposes of God, casting care to the wind, and advancing the kingdom of the King wheresoever He wished, even in remote places no one else cared about. Except God.

13

The Transplanters: Cassian and Germanus

At first, it was a few. Then it was hundreds. And by the fifth century, it was tens of thousands. A rain of righteousness was bringing thousands to the ninth door—to connect daily with the love of God.

Yes, they were discovering the "hallway with nine doors"—that is, the eight false doors that Christians must shun if we want to gain consistent access to the Door, Jesus. If you could consistently, daily, go through that "Jesus-Door" into the presence of God, He would pour His love into you. Then His love would transform you, and you could be a conduit of His love to other people. This was new—a power flowing from the cross of Jesus. This was real. This was the kingdom of God. This would transform the world.

At that time, God led two men directly out of the Egyptian desert to transplant into the Celtic garden what had been growing in the desert hot-house of prayer.

Starting in Bethlehem and Syria, these two men toured the desert together at the end of the fourth century, just as Rome was thinking about self-destructing. They sat at the feet of Pachomius, Evagrius, and many other Desert Fathers. Then the enemy brought conflict, accusation, and unpleasantness into Egypt. On top of it all, Evagrius died at age fifty-five, a painful death, unlike the long-lasting Antony. There was much that these two men saw that brought them back down to grim reality.

So these two desert pilgrims decided to leave the deserts of Egypt to spend the rest of their lives in Gaul among the Celts. The older of them, Germanus, became Germanus of Auxerre and established a famous school. His younger side-kick, John Cassian, moved to Marseilles to start two houses of prayer, one for men, the other for women.

Germanus of Auxerre

As for Germanus, his school became the most influential school of his day for Celtic Westerners. He became the most important disseminator of the pattern of kingdom living to both the Irish and the Welsh houses of prayer that would soon grow up to transform Celtic tribes. Not only did many of the future leaders of the Celtic prayer movement attend Germanus' school, but he made two trips to Britain, one in 429, the other in the mid-430s, to help the Celts get well-grounded.

Germanus and Cassian became skilled at leading people down "the hallway with nine doors." What these men were dealing with was this: it is one thing to help a small circle of intimates down that hallway. But it is much more difficult to lead great crowds, such as became interested in Jesus during their generation. We don't know exactly what Germanus taught in his school because we have no records. But we do know what Cassian taught in his house of prayer because his writings are preserved and can easily be read today.

His main two books are the *Institutes,* and the *Conferences,* both of which set forth his principles for prayer communities. That is, *for churches*—because to Cassian, the Church *is* a house of prayer. And this is the concept that the Celts will be running with in future centuries. It is important to remember that Cassian had absolutely no experience with church buildings full of pews, pulpits, stained glass windows, and steeples. Any ideas like this are going to get in the way of appreciating what God was recommending as "normal Christianity" during these first seven centuries. Cassian's two books would become guiding beacons in the Celtic world right on through the eighth century. So it is important for us to lay hold of the foundations he laid down, foundations built into his own life by the Desert Fathers and Mothers.

Cassian's Principles for Communities

Let's look at Cassian's principles for the kingdom of God. We can assume the same was true for Germanus, not only because they had walked together and learned together from all the same teachers, but because Cassian constantly mentions Germanus in his writings for having learned those same lessons with him.

To begin with, Cassian defines the kingdom of God. His goal is not to spread religion but to help people discover the kingdom. He writes: "The aim of our profession is the kingdom of God or the kingdom of heaven. But our point of reference, our objective, is a clean heart, without which it is impossible for anyone to reach our target." Purity of heart is the objective, while eternal life is the goal.[50] Cassian would have thought our idea of just wanting to "go to heaven after you die" completely unbiblical. The whole idea is to live as citizens of the kingdom of heaven, as the Bible teaches. And that requires us to hear all the other things Jesus taught, besides how to "get to heaven." He believed in the whole counsel of God. And the purpose of the kingdom, after all, is to bring heaven to earth. "On earth as it is in heaven."

The kingdom of God, according to Cassian, happens when people connect with God out of a pure heart and gain the ability to love. But when dealing with a lot of people, this task becomes complicated. Antony had it easy, just going off by himself into the desert. But a great many people had, by now, tried to do what Antony did—and failed! Cassian had seen them go off into the desert, fall under the deception of the evil one, and kill themselves! Or teach bizarre doctrines or do other bizarre things.

So Cassian is having to back up and figure out what is going wrong and come up with answers. He sees that extreme severity to the body is not what is producing the kingdom of God, as you might have thought at first from reading about Antony. So you hear Cassian talking about "excessive and inappropriate fasting."[51] Instead of just adopting extreme severity to the body, you have to discern God's heart. You have to learn to listen to Him and discern His voice from the very clever counterfeits of the evil one.

Cassian has also grown skeptical about extreme solitude—people going out on their own into the desert without a good deal of training and help from a community of believers. So he counsels us to spend at least two years learning from experienced believers before attempting a life of solitude. No person should just read a book (like *The Life of Antony*) and then go out and try to do what Antony did. Everyone needs a discipleship community. Everyone needs some elders, some Christian believers who have already gained years of experience and can then help new believers know the ropes. This is what Cassian believes is the true role of the Church. Disciple-making.

Cassian's Principles for Living

Owen Chadwick describes the legacy of Cassian in his Introduction to the *Conferences*. Let me summarize his introduction. Why are these ideas important? Because these are the ideas that will successfully transform the British Isles. We want to understand how Christianity replaced paganism in those early years. Kingdom transformation took place by means of a By-My-Spirit lifestyle and disciple-making evangelism. What did that look like?

Cassian's goal is to take the bits and pieces of wisdom he gained in the desert and work them into a coherent scheme of spirituality that would be useful for all people. The goal of Christian maturity cannot be won in a moment; it takes years. But God has given us years, so let us use them for the purpose of becoming Christlike.

1. Friendships

To begin with, a very important method God wants to use in attaining this goal is *friendships*—the very thing that Cassian and Germanus had going for them. "With Germanus, he (Cassian) sat at the feet of the holy men of Egypt. He felt that he owed a lasting debt to a close personal friendship with Germanus, and this friendship rested on a common moral aim."[52] This idea—that friendship is an important tool God uses in bringing us to maturity—is going to be vastly important among the Celts. They are going to take this idea of friendship and run with it as far as they can go. They will call it *soul friendship*. Look for this in the pages below.

2. Private Prayer, or Public?

Cassian struggled with what the Bible recommends with regard to prayer: should it be private or public? Some praying Christians said that you should be part of a community that comes together seven times a day, based on Psalm 119:164: "Seven times a day I praise you for your righteous laws." Others followed the words of Jesus, to go into your room by yourself and shut the door (Matthew 6:6). Both of these Biblical verses were important seeds of inspiration to early believers. But each had its dangers. Few new believers had the discipline to know what to do when they went into their room and shut the door. Most young people would simply end up daydreaming and wasting time. On the other hand, when believers came together to recite psalms and pray together, the thing tended to spin into empty religion, just going through the motions.

Cassian "was always aware of the prayer of the secret heart as taking precedence over the prayer of the lips."[53] With Cassian, the goal was always to help a person actually connect with God in private so that his or her public prayer would be an outgrowth of deep love nurtured in private. "Cassian accepted and used corporate prayer. But he was a man of private prayer."[54] And his goal was very much to help people "pray without ceasing" (1 Thessalonians 5:17).

3. Miracles?

Cassian also had to deal with the amazing miracles and healings that God would do among praying people. Owen Chadwick comments:

Part of fanaticism was miracle-hunting. A people's wonder was easily evoked by the marvelous and easily credited. Miracle-workers won crowds of followers. Cassian did not doubt that miracles happen. Sometimes they are evidence of holiness.... You are never to admire men who put themselves forward as miracle-workers or healers or exorcists. Only admire them for charity. See if they love. Cassian records some marvels, but his object was to show how they arose out of compassion, how the aim was not ostentation but charity. ...Humility and charity are always necessary. Miracles are not always necessary.[55]

4. Spiritual and Intellectual Elitism

Cassian was rooted in prayer, but he did not want prayer to become elitist. Cassian wanted to give spirituality a stable base and not to let it soar so high that prayer loses touch with real men and women. Jesus died so that all men and women would be able to connect with God. So part of the challenge was to disciple people, ordinary people so that real prayer is diffused into societies. A priesthood not of the few but of everyone.

Nor did he want to see the prayer movement become an ivory tower exercise for intellectuals.

Cassian also was a bit skeptical of the role of the human mind, of scholarship per se. Cassian had something more anti-intellectual than some of his successors. He allowed that a mind could and should study, in the academic sense of study. But he was afraid of it, at least in the young. Academic study, at least in the young, easily led to pride in knowledge, or to a vanity that made a young man speak too quickly....

The illiterate is as capable of penetrating the deepest truths as is the mind of encyclopedic learning.[56]

5. Our Desperate Need of God

Cassian had a deep awareness of the weakness of human effort, and at the base of all his prayer strategy was a reliance on the grace and power of God. This is because he saw that demons are greater than we are; they are more deceptive than most people realize, and only by God's mercy can we rise above their influence. Because demons are so powerful and persistent, the soul is always at the mercy of God. It is helpless without His help. Man is free to choose. You must exercise your moral judgment. You must try. You must discipline yourself. But still, the soul is helpless without God. The grace of God must help you to begin, continue, and end. Purity of heart is a gift, not an achievement. Still, you must try.[57]

6. Monastic Rules?

What about monastic rules, such as those that came into popularity with the Benedictines two centuries later? Is it possible to reduce the whole life of prayer to a single set of rules that would lay out the way of the kingdom for everyone? Cassian thought not. Even though his *Institutes* sets forth principles to help ordinary people connect with God,

Cassian did not yet organize a rule, nor even have the idea of a written rule.

Under God, the soul is free. But it will not be truly free unless it follows the hard-won experience of the Fathers.... The atmosphere of Cassian is not one of legal obedience to legally appointed authority. It is one of discipleship to a wise and holy master and therefore acceptance of his advice.[58]

Discipleship is a human art flowing from a human heart. It cannot be replaced by words on paper, nor rules and schedules in a monastic system.

7. The Church as a House of Prayer

Owen Chadwick finishes with an appraisal of the tension between the quest of the monk, and the ordinary life of churches such as we have today, as reflected in Cassian's writings:

The individual experience of the divine is overwhelming. It passes beyond the memory of biblical texts and every other thought. Does it also pass beyond sacraments? Or sermons? If wordless apprehension is the highest, what need of congregations, where babies cry, and dogs bark, and young men ogle, and priests show off their voices, and old widows commit superstition? Might it be that holy anarchy is nearer to God than ordered ecclesiasticism? A monk is nothing but a simple Christian heart trying to find his Maker. Why does he need a church to intrude on his privacy, which is an experience of God unique to himself and incapable of being shared with another?[59]

Neither John Cassian nor Owen Chadwick offers clear answers to this question. The fifth century is too soon for answers to emerge. Chadwick comments: "He did not settle the great problem—the link between the Church and the monasteries within the Church—which was to stay with the

Church through all the centuries, never quite solved, until settled so fiercely by the Reformation in northern Europe...."[60]

Kingdom Principles Ready for the Garden

Our interest is to show how Cassian and Germanus influenced the ancient Celtic Church. And I wish simply to point out that Chadwick's summary of Cassian's writings is an exact description of Christian practice as taught by the next eight generations of Celtic leaders. Cassian and Germanus effectively transplanted the By-My-Spirit pattern from the deserts of Egypt to the Celtic lands of the far west, even to the tiniest islands of Ireland and Scotland.

If I might summarize the basic awareness of kingdom reality that they took from the desert and transplanted into Britain, it is this. Satan superintends the world, and it will continue to be so until Jesus returns at the end of the age and casts him down "so that he can deceive the world no longer" (Revelation 20:3). In the meantime, we have to deal with a being who is far more powerful, clever, and deceptive than we can possibly imagine. The only hope we have to rise above him and achieve a life of victory is to appropriate for ourselves what happened when Jesus died on the cross. Otherwise, we are toast.

These leaders put absolutely no confidence in the ability of the human race to evolve into something good. The number of lies that can be traced to a satanic origin is beyond counting. The cross of Christ alone is where we can find the Truth of who God is and how we can walk in His victory. The "deadly thoughts" of Evagrius and Cassian were simply their attempt to provide generic humanity with some handles to sidestep the obvious deceptions of the evil one so that we may stay pure, productive, and positive about life.

Out of the Cross, too, will be found our destiny, which Jesus distributes as Sovereign Lord of History. Each of us has a unique destiny, "created in Christ Jesus for good works" that He has planned for us from before we were formed in the womb (Ephesians 2:10). By drawing near to God, we discover not only God but our own true selves.

14

The First Western Awakening

In the following chapters, I want to show a great awakening, the spiritual awakening that brought virtually all of the British Isles out of paganism and into the love of Jesus. It transformed British culture, as Thomas Cahill described the Irish transformation under Patrick, which was the center of it (but not the beginning).

> *This thirty-year span of Patrick's mission in the middle of the fifth century encompasses a period of change so rapid and extreme that Europe will never see its like again. By 461, the likely year of Patrick's death, the Roman Empire is careening in chaos, barely fifteen years away from the death of the last western emperor. The accelerated change is, at this point, so dramatic we should not be surprised that the eyes of historians have been riveted on it or that they have failed to notice a transformation just as dramatic—and even more abrupt—taking place at the empire's periphery. For as the Roman lands went from peace to chaos, the land of Ireland was rushing even more rapidly from chaos to peace.*[61]

Ray Simpson puts it more simply: "This was perhaps the greatest period of blessing and growth in the history of Christianity."[62]

If it wasn't Rome just spreading the One True Religion to the West, as most people have believed, our question about this great transformation is: What *did* God do? How did this major spiritual awakening happen? And this will be an important clue to answering the larger question: How do all spiritual awakenings occur? How does the kingdom of God advance throughout the world? Surely the first of these spiritual awakenings, for Westerners at least, would hold important clues for us today?

Holy Grails

The search for the spiritual fortunes of Christ has produced a great many red herrings that have led spiritual fortune hunters on many, many wild goose chases. Consider Joseph of Arimathea, who, it was said, had come from Jerusalem to Britain in the first century, bearing with him the actual chalice that had held the blood of Jesus as it spilled out from the broken body of the dying Savior. This has produced generations of holy grail hunters throughout the centuries, not to mention scholars who have looked for evidence of Joseph of Arimathea in British history.

This is not to say that Joseph didn't come to Britain, bringing his chalice with him. Only that all searches for Joseph, his chalice (and the hoped-for miracles and Nirvanas that would occur if only the grail could be located) have yielded nothing, after centuries of searching."[63] Or just this: they have produced a lot of income for Hollywood directors and novelists dreaming up films and books about the Holy Grail. Even Adolf Hitler had his try.

The search for the holy grail and for any objective information about Joseph reminds me of the wistfulness of the Jewish exiles trying to rebuild the temple in Jerusalem while mourning the absence of the holy objects that had graced the temple of Solomon. Whereupon the prophet Haggai[64] pointed them to the future coming of the Desire of Nations—the Messiah—and advised them not to waste time looking for the relics of the past. A great deal of time has been wasted looking for "the holy grail." But, beginning with Ninian, the real search was for the kingdom of God, not for grails and relics.

I believe that the By-My-Spirit pattern that eventually spread throughout the British Isles is a far more worthwhile treasure to look for. "Seek first the Kingdom of God and His righteousness" (Matthew 6:33), Jesus said—and that is just what we see in Ninian, Cassian, and Germanus, and those who looked to them as mentors.

Whatever Joseph of Arimathea may have done in the first century, we will probably never know. But archaeologists do confirm the presence of Ninian at Whithorn, and I believe that he was the real root of the spiritual awakening of the British Isles—a root fertilized by Cassian and Germanus. The patterns that were started by Ninian, relying on the power and presence of God in the Holy Spirit, were the patterns that continued right through the seventh century until virtually all of Britain had given up on paganism and came to embrace Jesus Christ. It was as though a "good infection" (as C. S. Lewis used to call it) had started at Whithorn, and you can trace the spread to Ireland, also down to Wales, then to Cornwall and Brittany, back north to Argyll in Scotland, then to Northumberland and the rest of England. So we are going to count Ninian as the First Generation, even though, yes, there will be some Christians already in Britain, of whom we know almost nothing.

God was bringing "a time of refreshing from the presence of the Lord," made possible by the death of Jesus, who opened the door to authoritative Christian prayer. The importance of that death resided in the authority Jesus was giving people who were surrendering their lives to Him and inviting the Holy Spirit to lead them into a kingdom adventure.

Intensive prayer, stirred by the Holy Spirit, brings the presence of God, which invites ministries of discipling, and the pattern of sound teaching in the Word. This is the pattern we learn from the ancient Celtic Church.

There. I have said it. Now let's look at how God transformed the British Isles.

15

GENERATION TWO: PATRICK

Strange, the fickleness of memory. As we move from Ninian to Patrick, we transition from one of the least remembered to surely the most remembered of all these ancient saints. And yet, what we have "remembered" about Patrick is almost entirely untrue. More than that: the things Patrick wanted us to remember about him—his encounters with the power and presence of God in the transformation of Ireland—are the one thing about him that we have not remembered.

Humility works against history. Most of the Christians of this ancient period never left records of their own lives because they felt it would be prideful to do so. Patrick is the one exception to this rule: at the end of his life, he wrote a brief biography—a defense of his life work. And the only reason he did this was to answer criticism for his leadership. We don't know who was castigating him or for what. But the criticism led him to write the story of his life in his own words. Some of the most criticized people in world history have been men and women who walked with God so effectively that God entrusted them to lead great Revival movements.

His book, *The Confession of Saint Patrick*, alternately titled *Patrick on the Great Works of God*, shows us that, in telling his story, Patrick just wanted to brag on God. His biographical stories are, therefore, some of the best contemporary evidence of the power of God in the transformation of Western nations like Ireland.

Will the Real Patrick Please Stand Up

It may surprise some that Patrick himself was not Irish but a Welshman (Briton).[65] No one knows exactly where he was born, but most scholars seem to place him somewhere in the region of Strathclyde, between Dumbarton and Carlisle.[66]

The importance of Strathclyde is that it is the region that had been evangelized by Ninian. Patrick's parents were Christians—though as a teenager, he had not embraced the faith in any personal way. But he had been exposed to it, growing up in a Christian household. The Patrick connection to Strathclyde would help explain why later generations of Christians felt such a strong sense of spiritual attachment to this region. Ninian's Whithorn (like Martin's Marmoutier) were the most frequent places of pilgrimage to honor Celtic Christian roots.[67]

Assuming that Patrick grew up under Ninian's influence, that makes Patrick "Generation Two" of the Celtic awakening, as we attempt to trace the flow from one generation to the next. But he himself was not aware of this flow at the time because he had not yet embraced Christ at the ripe old age of 16. We today have the benefit of hindsight.

Before Patrick had a chance to say yes or no to God, the Irish (under the high king, Niall of the Nine Hostages) captured Patrick on a slave raid and carried him off to Ireland, where he was expected to tend sheep. According to a later biographer, [68] his master was Miliucc, a minor Irish king in the region of Cruithni on a mountain called Sliab Mis.

But the odd thing was that from the moment he was turned into an Irish shepherd, Patrick found himself overwhelmed by what might be called a spirit of grace and supplication.[69] This was an act of God, pure and simple. God was using Patrick to do something in Ireland that needed getting done. And Patrick was willing. This is how Patrick himself described the experience:

But then, when I had arrived in Ireland and was spending every day looking after flocks, I prayed frequently each day. And more and more, the love of God and the fear of him grew [in me] and [my] faith was increased and [my] spirit was quickened, so that in a day I prayed up to a hundred times, and almost as many in the night. Indeed, I even remained in the wood and on the mountain to pray. And— come hail, rain, or snow—I was up before dawn to pray, and I sensed nothing of evil nor any other spiritual laziness in me. I now understand why this was so; at that time "the Spirit was fervent" in me.

And it was there indeed that one night I heard a voice which said to me: "Well have you fasted. Very soon you are to travel to your homeland.[70]

Even though Patrick didn't count himself as a Christian, there was something already operating in his life so that he knew how to pray. Here is where I believe the spiritual influence of Ninian can first be seen. Patrick prayed and fasted for seven years for Ireland in the sheep-pastures of Miliucc. At the end of seven years, God wonderfully provided for him to escape, and he eventually found his way back home.

His parents pleaded with him not to leave them again. But one day, after a few years, Patrick had the following experience:

"I saw a vision of the night": a man named Victoricus—
"like one" from Ireland—coming with innumerable letters.
He gave me one of them and I began to read what was in
it: "The voice of the Irish." And at that very moment as I
was reading out the letter's opening, I thought I heard the
voice of those around the wood of Foclut, which is close to
the western sea. It was "as if they were shouting with one
voice": "O holy boy, we beg you to come again and walk
among us." And I was "broken hearted" and could not read
anything more. And at that moment I woke up.

...And on another occasion, I saw him praying in me,
and it was as if I was inside my body and I heard [him]
over me, that is over "the inner man," and he was praying
there powerfully with sighs. And in my excitement and
astonishment I wondered who it could be that was praying
in me. But toward the end of the prayer it became clear that
it was the Spirit.[71]

Sensing that God had a destiny for him among the Irish,
he came to realize that his whole experience of slavery had a
purpose in it. Again, in his own words: "But this [captivity]
was very good for me for I was corrected by the Lord; and he
prepared me for what I am today...."[72]

To say that the captivity was, in the end, a good thing is
an understatement. The experience gave Patrick a distaste for
slavery so that he became the first man in world history to oppose
slavery, setting up the first abolition movement that spread
throughout the ancient Celtic Church. As Thomas Cahill put
it, "The greatness of Patrick is beyond dispute; the first human
being in the history of the world to speak out unequivocally

against slavery. Nor will any voice as strong as his be heard again till the seventeenth century."[73] —A good example of how King Jesus turns a curse into a blessing. Generations of Irish leaders will work for the abolition of slavery, and the abolition of slavery will become a mark of certain Revival movements well into the future. Jesus Christ is the same, yesterday, today, and forever.

The Call to Ireland

According to Muirchù, Patrick's main biographer, he left for Rome to receive training in ministry, but he was side-tracked and ended up with Germanus of Auxerre, who trained him and sent him out. In the meantime, Rome had sent someone else, Palladius, archdeacon under Pope Celestine, but this official apostle made no headway among the Irish and, according to Muirchù, "Palladius did not want to spend long in a land not his own. So he decided to return to Pope Celestine."[74] This opened the way for Patrick, who went with a presbyter, Segitius, to bring the Irish to a knowledge of the King of Love. This put Patrick right in the middle of an intense spiritual battle.

Confronting the Dark Powers

Niall's son was now on the throne, and Muirchù gives us a little background about what was already happening behind the scenes, just prior to Patrick's arrival:

The king was Loiguire, son of Niall, whose family ruled almost the whole island. He had with him seers and wise men and augurs and spell-casters and those skilled in every one of the evil arts....Two of these were preferred by the king above the rest: Lothrock...and Lucet Mael....

With their magical skill, this pair often declared that they could see another way of life about to come to Ireland from outside. It would be like a kingdom, it would come from far away across the seas, and it would bring an unknown and annoying teaching with it. This teaching would be given out by a handful, yet be received by many, and held in honor by all. It would overthrow kingdoms, kill the kings who resisted it, seduce the crowds, destroy all their gods, cast out their own skills and works, and this kingdom would have no end. They also pointed to the man who would bring this new way of life and persuade people [to accept it]. They prophesied in words that made up a kind of poem which was often received in those days, and especially in the two or three years just before Patrick's coming.[75]

Kingdom Prophecies

So we can imagine that word had gotten around in Ireland because this poem about an intruding kingdom had circulated widely. And we can imagine that people were wondering about it. Then Patrick showed up.[76] This story of local, indigenous prophecy given in advance of the intrusion of the Gospel of the kingdom into Ireland may seem fantastic, and yet the advance of the Gospel of the kingdom through the ages is full of just such stories among the nations, and I will tell some of them in Volume Two. In fact, I tell these stories precisely to establish patterns that keep appearing again and again in the global narrative of the kingdom of God.

Patrick's first idea, upon arrival, was to go to the local king he had served for seven years and buy himself out of slavery.

So he was eager to go to the northern regions and find the pagan Miliucc, who had held him captive. He brought with him twice the price of his servitude, namely the heavenly and the earthly, that he might free the man he once served as a slave.[77]

Entering the area, he was met by one man who remembered Patrick and engaged him in conversation. This man was quickly converted to the Christian faith. Patrick then went on to meet Miliucc to buy himself out of slavery and to share the gospel with his former master. "But Miliucc heard that his slave was coming to see him to make him, by force as it were, change his ways. He did not want this at the end of his life as he did not want to become a subject to his former servant, nor that the servant should now rule over him. At the devil's prompting, he decided to destroy himself by fire. So he gathered all his possessions in the house where he was once a king and set fire to them and himself."[78]

Here we see the satanic strategy of the poem that had been circulating—to create false impressions and fear of a Power-and-Might kingdom forcing itself on all Irish. Patrick, approaching this burning mansion, stood speechless in the presence of the tragedy. Imagine his sadness at this turn of events!

If Patrick had thought it would be easy to bring the Irish into the love of Jesus, he was now certainly aware that he was thrown right into the middle of a spiritual battle. It looks as though he was given help in the form of a personal angel, Victoricus, who would meet with him, giving him personal instruction on how to proceed. He would surely need angelic help, considering that the kingdom of God was about to overspread the entire nation of Ireland. And so it came to this: There was a power encounter.

Confrontation

The palace of King Loiguire, son of Niall, was located at Tara, and the great annual feast of the Druids happened to coincide with the Passover, which was to be celebrated by Patrick on the plains of Tara. So Patrick chose to celebrate the Passover within sight of the king's palace on the hill. But there was a problem: according to custom, anyone who lit a fire prior to the official fire on this festival night would be put to death. Patrick's fire, by which he was celebrating the Passover, was visible to everyone on the plains of Tara—and Patrick had no intention of dousing his fire. As Muirchù tells it, it was a direct challenge to the king and the pagan counselors around him.

Muirchù goes on to describe a lengthy series of encounters between the King and his counselors on one side, and Patrick on the other, in which Patrick prevails in every case. Muirchù's "Life of Patrick" goes on for several pages describing these encounters, which look like they may have been exaggerated to show parallels with Moses and Elijah in the Bible.

On the other hand, when you examine the front edge of kingdom advance throughout history, you often find stories like this. Scholars, ensconced in their private studies, surrounded by books, may think that it's all just "legends." But let them view the DVDs that George Otis and Darren Wilson have been putting out, [79] and they will see incredible stories in our own time, at the front edge of kingdom advance. Let the stories of today speak to the stories of yesterday, and *vice versa*. They help us establish kingdom paradigms in our worldview. Jesus Christ is the same yesterday, today, and forever.

The Story of a Highway Robber

Let me finish, then, with the much briefer story of MacCuill Graeccae, which is compact enough to include here, just to show Patrick's way of confronting wickedness and rescuing people from the grip of the evil one. MacCuill was a highway robber, and there is a special place in the history of the kingdom of God for such as these. MacCuill occupied a mountain fortress called Druim moccu Echach, from which he and his band of merry men would ambush and kill unwary travelers. "Cyclops" was the nickname given to him by the locals.

One day, Patrick came wandering by on "their" highway. They recognized him as the Christian who was turning their country upside down, and they came up with a scheme to show him as the charlatan they believed him to be. They quickly assigned one of their number to pretend he was deathly ill. Then MacCuill went out and asked Patrick to come and pray for the "sick man." Patrick, of course, had already heard of them, and there is every indication that he knew from the start that something was amiss. Entering the dwelling, Patrick replied to the invitation with these unexpected words: "If he had been ill, his death would be no surprise."

Startled by Patrick's retort, the gang investigated and discovered that the man in the bed was, in fact, dead. The gang was all dumbfounded. Patrick replied, "Why did you want to tempt me?" Realizing that their scheme had gone terribly wrong and stricken with remorse, MacCuill repented of the whole scheme—seems to have repented of the whole course of his life. He agreed to listen to Patrick and submitted to do whatever Patrick would tell him. Patrick invited him to believe in Jesus, confess his sins, and be baptized. And he did.

He confessed the worst—that he had intended to kill Patrick, and he unfolded his whole life before him. Then he concluded: "Judge what is the debt that I owe for so great a crime."

Patrick replied:

> *I am unable to judge, but God will judge. You must now go down to the sea, unarmed, and leave this part of Ireland. You can take none of your riches except one piece of clothing. Something poor and small which just about covers you. You are not to taste or drink any of the fruits of this island, and you shall bear this as a mark of your sin upon your head. When you arrive at the shore, bind your feet with an iron fetter and throw its key into the sea. Then get into a one-hide boat and put to sea without a rudder or an oar. You can then accept wherever the wind and sea take you. In whichever place divine Providence lands you, there you are to…keep God's commandments.*[80]

MacCuill did exactly what Patrick commanded and allowed this notoriously unstable craft—the one-hide Irish coracle—to carry him away from Ireland to the Isle of Man, which had just gained two bishops, named Conindrus and Rumilus. These two men "happened" to be in a position to see MacCuill arrive. They took him in and discipled him—and eventually, MacCuill became the next bishop on the Isle of Man.

A Little Summary of a Great Man

All the evidence points to two major accomplishments in Patrick's ministry that helped to bring Ireland from a pagan to a Christian nation in his lifetime: He possessed a breaker anointing that smashed the power of the demonic realm over

Ireland, and he established the first system of bishops throughout the country so that there would be mutual accountability and visible unity among Christians. The patterns of By-My-Spirit Christianity spread out over Ireland to completely change the atmosphere of the country in a very short time.

As Patrick himself testified. And, as we shall see.

16

THIRD GENERATION: BRIGID

One of the early converts that Patrick baptized was a woman who had been captured from among the Picts, just as he had been captured from the Britons of Strathclyde as a teenager. Her name was Brocca, and she had a daughter, Brigid, named after a pagan goddess. Brigid grew up in a Druid household and received a traditional Irish education (women were considered equal to men and worthy of education). She was a young girl during the final years of Patrick's life, and the two developed a warm friendship. Brigid may thus be considered the third generation in this Celtic awakening. (She died in the year 523, sixty years after Patrick's death.)

Brigid quickly moved into a position of leadership and was honored ever after as being equal in stature to Patrick. From the Book of Armagh:

> Between St Patrick and St Brigid, the pillars of the Irish people, there was so great a friendship of charity that they had but one heart and one mind. Through him and through her, Christ performed many great works.[81]

Unfortunately, her biographers give us almost no useful information about her true accomplishments. The various "Lives of Brigid" are nothing but a string of miracle stories, one after another. But it is obvious that her leadership was influential in many other ways, and we wish we could have glimpsed the true secrets of her leadership more fully. It was Brigid, more than anyone, who took Patrick's powerful beginnings and, like Cassian, developed them into a pattern which could be—and was—imitated again and again throughout Ireland. She did this not by drawing up a "Rule of St. Brigid" but by simply providing a personal example of good leadership, which other people wanted to follow.

She also developed a school of the arts, focused especially on biblical manuscript illumination. The Book of Kildare became legendary for its beauty and artistry—but unfortunately, the book has since been lost. Yet the art of manuscript illumination became an enduring legacy of the Celtic awakening we are describing, and, to be frank, it shows a love for the Word of God rarely equaled since that time.

Most important, perhaps, were the houses of prayer she founded, one for men, the other for women, at Kildare. To help her lead them, she brought in a hermit named Conleth, and the two of them demonstrated the possibility of a man and a woman being "subject one to another out of reverence for Christ" (Ephesians 5:21) in effective Christian leadership.

Contextualizing the Gospel

Brigid's beginnings bring up an issue that must be addressed before I go any further, so let me describe her method of establishing the house of prayer at Kildare:

> *St Bridget's first convent was built on the Liffey plain at Kildare, on land given to her by her friend the King of Leinster. It was on the site of an ancient pagan sanctuary*

marked by a large oak tree. Indeed, the name Kildare means "Church of the Oak Tree," and in time, it became the principal church of the kingdom.[82]

Given the fact that she never changed her name after she became a Christian and founded her house of prayer on the site of a pagan sanctuary, some have suggested that the whole Celtic Church was forever polluted by Celtic paganism. In other words, they are saying that it is an example of syncretism—mixing Christianity and paganism in a mass of confusion. Of course, this is exactly what New Agers want to believe. But is it true?

Syncretism vs. Contextualization

Let's press the Pause button for just a moment and take stock of what was really happening here. It was the apostle Paul who established the principle of contextualizing the Gospel, as he first bridged the cultural divide between Jews and Gentiles. Paul had gained God's views about this during his time in the wilderness prior to embarking on his God-given apostolic ministry, which he described in Galatians 1:11-24. It was here, in the desert, that Paul was able to tap into God's thoughts. As a result, he learned to become all things to all people, that he might by all possible means save some. (See 1 Corinthians 9:19-23.) Paul built bridges to other, non-Jewish cultures by walking across to the other side of the cultural gap and by not requiring that Gentiles become Jews before becoming Christians. Paul defended this stance at the Council at Jerusalem (Acts 15). So contextualizing the Gospel has strong biblical roots.

The Chinese pioneer missionary Hudson Taylor famously applied this same principle to English missions during the 19th century as he contextualized the Gospel to inland China. To howls of ridicule from other English Christians, he began to dress Chinese and adopt other Chinese ways in building a bridge between English and Chinese cultures for the sake of the Gospel. Taylor was reclaiming the principle of "becoming all things to all people in order to save some," and Christian missionaries have followed this principle ever since.

Over the last twenty-five years, I have been privileged to take part in the contextualizing of the Gospel to Native Americans. For many years, we white Christians have insisted that American and Canadian tribes learn our culture on the way to becoming Christians. This mistaken approach— the uncontextualized Gospel—produced "Indian boarding schools," a terrible modern example of Power-and-Might Christianity, full of child abuse, which only convinced many Native people that Christianity is "the white man's religion"— not for them.

But since the 1990s, there has emerged a contextualizing movement in which a new generation of Native leaders have reached out to the tribes with the message, "You can be fully Christian and fully Native at the same time." The late Richard Twiss established Wiconi Ministries to proclaim the new message by his "Many Nations One Voice" conferences. (My wife and I attended the first one, the only white attendees present.) These conferences birthed a movement. My friends, Jonathan Maracle (Mohawk) and Bill Pagaran (Tlingit) are taking a contextualized Gospel all over "Indian country" and seeing hundreds welcome Jesus as Lord and Savior. This approach has been vastly more effective than denominational ministries that plant Western "churches" with their pulpits, pews and stained-glass windows, and a picture of white Jesus behind the pulpit.

Contextualized ministry involves a Holy Spirit sifting and discerning as to which practices in a culture are inappropriate for a Christian to maintain without compromising his faith. Every time the Gospel moves from one culture to another, the apostle (or "sent out one") who takes it across that cultural bridge must try to discern between contextualism and syncretism—combining things with Christianity that don't belong there.

So now the question is: Did the Celts contextualize the Gospel properly, or did they add things to Christianity that didn't belong there? The answer is: they contextualized the Gospel properly. They were as orthodox as any Christians anywhere in the world. Let me simply quote the scholar, Bruce Ritchie, from his new book about the Irish founder of the Iona community, Columba, who represents the flower of the Irish Church:

> *The Irish Church was hard-wired into international Christendom, revering the Church Fathers of the Greek East and the Latin West. An older view which presumed that Ireland and its Church was cut off from wider European and Mediterranean civilization following the Anglo-Saxon invasions of Britain has been replaced by an awareness that the Irish Church continued to have strong links with the rest of the Christian world. The theological instruction which was given in Irish monasteries was the same as that offered in institutions offered all over*

Christendom. From the deserts of Egypt to the western shores of Europe, a common teaching was imparted.[83]

To summarize, the Celtic Church was as Biblical and orthodox as any church anywhere in the world. Enough said.

13

KINGDOM ADVANCE IN WALES

What began in Strathclyde could not be contained. This transformational kingdom was most notably transferred to Ireland, but it also went south.

Bear in mind that all of Britain was suffering from the loss of the Roman armies, which had kept a modicum of order among warring tribes and kingdoms. In addition, Anglo-Saxons had been invading Britain from northern Europe, settling the eastern half of what is today England, pushing the Celts to the West while taking some of them as slaves. And if the Arthurian scholars are right[84]—who began in the 1980s to point out that there may have been a king or general of that name who actually lived and who fought twelve battles between 467 and 516—then the Anglo-Saxons were stopped in their tracks during this period we are calling The Third Generation. There would have been an invisible red line stretching roughly from Southampton in the south to Berwick in the north, with Anglo-Saxons to the east and Celts to the west.

That would have created enough stability to permit free travel to the south from Strathclyde. And remember that the tribes of the north are moving southward and settling what we know today as Wales. (But in those days, the Celtic peoples were called Britons, and a nation called Wales did not exist.)

During this generation, the Britons built a prosperous society with famous schools that attracted scholars even from Ireland so that there was peace and easy communication north and south, and tribes that spoke variations of the Celtic lingo began to mix together in peaceful friendship. The Gospel of the kingdom spread among these Britons from Whithorn in the north and from Ireland. As Geoffrey Ashe puts it, "The blaze of Celtic genius which made the smaller island a beacon to dark-age Europe was possible because Arthur had kept the heathen at arm's length."[85] Providential peace for the sake of the kingdom of God? That is what I think.

Cadoc

Now let's look at what happened in England west of the red line.

Born at the end of the fifth century in Wales, Cadoc grew up in a family known for violence and bravado. His brother became one of the great robber barons of his time; his father was known for violent raids on other estates—not a promising beginning for Cadoc, and a glaring window into the grim reality of the dying pagan social order in Celt country.

On one occasion, Gwynllyw (his father, with the most unpronounceable name in world history) staged a raid with a band of warriors, during which he stole a cow from an Irish monk, Tathan, who had moved close by. Tathan, unafraid of Gwynllyw, demanded his cow back and, in so doing, earned the respect of the man who had taken it. Cadoc's father then decided to put Cadoc in Tathan's care, and that is how Cadoc grew up in a Christian environment in Caerwent.

As an adult, Cadoc refused to take charge of his father's small army but founded a monastery or house of prayer at Llancarfan. From there, he went to study in Ireland for three years, following which he went north to Strathclyde, where he founded a house of prayer at Cambuslang, just south of present-day Glasgow (and home to one of the great Revivals of the Great Awakening during the 1740s. See my chapter in Volume Two). Then, after further years in Wales, he went to Brittany (in today's France), where he spread the Gospel of the kingdom among Celts who had migrated earlier from Britain. You see how the Gospel of the kingdom was free to move north to south and also back and forth from Ireland. On the other hand, none of it was touching the Anglo-Saxons.

Illtyd

At some point in all this, Cadoc apparently had a run-in with an Arthurian soldier named Illtyd (or Illtud). Cadoc would spend time away from monastic duties as a hermit, and, one day, a band of soldiers, mercenaries under a local king, Paulinus, discovered him in the woods all by himself. They made fun of him and roughed him up while Illtyd, their leader, was away on an errand. Michael Mitton continues with one version of this story:

> *Eventually, Illtyd turned up and was appalled to see the way his soldiers were treating Cadoc. He drove them out of the old man's hut and fell on his knees, begging forgiveness....*
>
> *During the night, Illtyd began to reflect on his life. Cadoc's life was in such contrast to his own. Eventually he fell asleep and had a dream that an angel came to him and said, "Until now you have been a knight serving mortal kings; from now on, I want you to be a knight in the service of an immortal king, the King of all Kings." When he awoke in*

the morning, he was in no doubt that he now wanted to fight in God's army against the dark powers of Satan....[86]

Unfortunately, all we know about this man is that he started a school named Cor Tewdws at Llanilltud Fawr in Wales, which became the most famous school of its time in the Isles. At the center of its curriculum were prayer and spiritual warfare to match the calling of God on Illtyd's life. It was responsible for training several of the most famous and influential Christian leaders. Among these was David, who is regarded as the founder of the Welsh Church, and Samson of Dol, who planted the Gospel of the kingdom to the south, in Cornwall, and then Brittany.

Though there is little reliable documentation of Illtyd's life, let me quote historian Geoffrey Ashe on the influence of this man in the widespread awakening that was taking place among the Celts. Most of this information is from bits and snatches that historians glean in their researches.

The reborn Christianity of the Celts was now cut off from the Church on the European continent, and different in system and atmosphere, though not in doctrine. Its centres were rural monasteries instead of city sees, and its heads were abbots instead of bishops. Celtic community life was less binding on the individual than the Rule of St Benedict (would be). Each monk had his separate cell. All ate together and assembled for worship in a chapel, but they enjoyed some freedom of movement. They were not only priests and missionaries but teachers, doctors, farmers, and builders. Britain's religious renewal was primarily an upsurge of energy in Wales, and the work of one remarkable man, St. Illtud.

...His monks reclaimed land and pioneered an improved method of ploughing. Illtud became, in the words of Gildas... "the polished teacher of almost the whole of Britain."[87]

Of course, Gildas had a different definition of Britain in those days than ours today. He would have been referring to the "Britons," that is, the Celtic Westerners, not the Anglo-Saxon Easterners. Notice, too, that even though Geoffrey Ashe uses the word "religious," the revolution that is happening actually touches every area of life. Spiritual warfare is at the center of a new way of life that excludes nothing. God is helping them re-think *how to live*. No area of human existence remains untouched. The kingdom of God is transformational.

Under the stability provided by Arthur, increasingly, Christian leaders will be able to move from one center of spiritual vibrancy to another, comparing notes and spreading their new way of life into each other's territories, as Cadoc was doing. And, as Geoffrey Ashe describes, this type of Christianity is going to differ remarkably from that which Rome had been developing, in all but basic doctrine.

18

IRELAND, FOURTH GENERATION

Back in Ireland, things are growing by a power not human. If such a thing were to happen today, we would call it a great awakening. But the term had not been invented yet, nor had anyone started talking about transformational Revival. To those people, it was simply the kingdom of God advancing, prospering, and changing everything. Because it was so good, it attracted a great many people, and the prayer movement that was its empowering furnace prospered beyond all human reckoning.

During this fourth generation, the number of people starting houses of prayer or "praying churches" was simply astonishing. There is a website, Omnium Sanctorum Hiberniae.blogspot.com ("All the Saints of Ireland"). It lists the Irish saints of old and their various feast days. Every single day of the year has at least two or three names, and an introduction to each person is given on this site. All were people who made their mark in the spiritual transformation of Ireland at the beginning, and there are hundreds and hundreds of them. And that's just Ireland. We aren't even talking yet about Wales, Scotland, Cornwall, Brittany, or the outreach into Northumbria and the Anglo-Saxons and beyond! What started with Ninian and Patrick, two lonely but courageous souls planting kingdom seed will multiply again and again into a great army of prayer warriors. For that is how the kingdom of God is advanced. By prayer. Faithful, consistent, driving, Christ-motivated prayer. And the Irish Church, if it was nothing else, was a house of prayer.

You may have noticed by now that there was no clear distinction between "churches" and "monasteries." Today, historians have to use these terms loosely because communities of Christians spanned the whole range from one to the other, with every variation in between and hermits thrown in to boot. There was simply no one pattern that fit all.

It must also be said of those Irish: they knew how to make disciples who were imbued with the power of multiplication. If Jesus is King, then the purpose of the Church is to "make disciples, teaching people to obey Him." These two very simple ingredients, prayer, and disciple-making were what transformed Ireland and the rest of Celt country. The Church never allowed itself to become merely a religious institution, performing Sunday services.

Celts did not do basilicas, following the Roman pattern. Rome had contextualized the Gospel by fitting it into basilicas on Sundays. But Christians in Ireland adapted the Gospel to the mentoring culture that was already in Ireland. They called it fostering. So it did not take a big adjustment to apply Celtic traditions toward the Great Commission of the Church: "Go make disciples." Disciple-making was simply Christian fostering.

The Celts did not have apostles buried in a holy city, from which they claimed apostolic succession, as did the Romans. But they did have an apostolic succession nonetheless, based on disciples mentoring other disciples. Trace it. Jesus discipled

John, who discipled Polycarp of Smyrna, who discipled Irenaeus, who moved to Gaul and began to disciple the Celts in the second century. There was a direct discipleship link with John through many generations, which may be one reason the Celts felt more connected to John, whereas the Romans had established a link with Peter (who was buried in Rome). In many ways, John was "buried" inside the collective awareness of the Celtic people. It was not a religious connection established by doctrines about apostolic succession. It was a discipleship inheritance built by mentoring through the generations. This was their version of apostolic succession.

We have also seen that the Desert Fathers and Mothers were the spiritual parents of the Celtic Church, in a direct line through Martin, John Cassian, and Germanus of Auxerre. Just as the prayer warriors of the desert would gather younger believers around them and mentor them, that is exactly how the Celtic Church grew and multiplied. There wasn't a single basilica builder in the lot. They built discipleship communities.

The Celtic Pattern

Ray Simpson has worked out the patterns of the ancient Celtic Church.[88] Let's look at those patterns of what was considered normal Christianity, patterns that have been almost completely forgotten but which were profoundly effective in advancing the kingdom of God.

Normally, a single man or woman of prayer launched out into a new region, guided by the Holy Spirit. This had been the pattern of Ninian, and it provides us with one more clue where these Celts were getting their inspiration. Often, the prayer evangelist would choose the mouth of a river as the best place to begin, perhaps because they were into subsistence living, and the river was a source of food. He/she would pray intensively and would also begin reaching out with the love of Jesus, especially to the poor. As he did so, he would explain the Gospel of the kingdom to everyone who would listen. Sometimes, miracles and healings took place, which got peoples' attention, as had happened with Peter at the Gate Beautiful.

Sooner or later, this pioneer would gather together a small prayer team who wanted to learn how to pray as he did. His role now became a soul friend, an *anamchara*. It was understood that if you were going to follow Jesus, you would have a soul friend to help you. The saying attributed to Brigid was: "A person without a soul friend is like a body without a head."

The soul friend made a long-term commitment to the new believer. His purpose was to help a new believer deal with all the issues of life from the new vantage point, the vantage point of Christ, and the Word of God. The mature believer was to love the new believer into obedience to Jesus. As Paul said, "I became your father in Christ Jesus." The challenge was to love people into the kingdom, not to take authority over them because God had set you over them in an alleged hierarchy. The Celtic Church was not hierarchical.

At the center of the house of prayer, there would be a copy of the Bible, calligraphed letter by letter by hand on vellum. It was a ponderous volume that would stay anchored in the house of prayer. Ray Simpson describes this volume: "More than 100 animals were needed to produce one Psalter. A Northumbrian Bible, now in Florence, contains over 2000 pages of vellum and weighs about eighty pounds."[89]

The prayer evangelist would also have a traveling version of the Word of God, which consisted usually of the four Gospels and the Psalms. This would be carried in a satchel that protected it from wear and weather. Needless to say, these books were precious beyond measure because they were each printed by hand and consisted of the hides of many, many animals, carefully cured and hand-lettered. The Bible was the vision statement of every local "praying church." Celtic intercessors got to know every letter of the Bible intimately.

The soul-friend prayer evangelist would mentor this new team, and the team would grow into a small house of prayer. Pretty soon, the leader would be called an abbot or abbess (father or mother), a title borrowed from the Egyptian desert. As more people were added to the number, some would be assigned leadership roles in the house of prayer. Some might eventually be sent out to start the pattern all over again in a new region. Gradually, a whole village would grow up around the house of prayer. Ray Simpson calls these "villages of God."[90]

Finnian of Clonard

One of the greatest leaders in the fourth generation in Ireland was Finnian of Clonard (470-549 AD). Finnian studied first at Marmoutier (though Martin had died a century before), then at Cadoc's school in Wales. Returning to Ireland after many years, he was further mentored at Brigid's house of prayer at Kildare. Finally, he started his own house of prayer, having been led by an angel to the River Boyne, where he spent the rest of his life building a school for Christian disciples.

The influence of this one man on the Irish Church was incalculable. In time, his school would train 3000 students in the ways of Christ. Before he was done, he had sent out from

Clonard "the Twelve Apostles of Ireland," who became some of the most famous world-changers of their day.[91]

Finnian took much of his teaching directly from Cassian, so the "hallway with nine doors"[92] was taught at the bottom level, based on Cassian's *Institutes* (who borrowed his ideas from Evagrius). In addition to simply forsaking the eight deadly thoughts on our way to the Door of Jesus, Finnian taught his students how to overcome evil with good. So he proposed virtues as antidotes to the poisons of the eight deadly thoughts. His book, *The Penitential of Finnian*, is the closest thing we have to a rule to be followed by Irish monasteries.

Finnian's school had three basic goals:

1. to cultivate purity of heart, which is the main hallmark of the kingdom of God;

2. to teach people to walk in the power of the Holy Spirit, the source of kingdom power; and

3. to help people pray without ceasing, thus becoming God's Royal Priesthood, even when doing menial tasks.

Finnian was known for his fierce passion for righteousness. The Irish flocked to him in droves because of it. Righteousness had become popular, a new normal. People were attracted to his fierce purity. Why? How did this happen?

Let me suggest two reasons.

First, God was on the move in answer to prayer. We will see this pattern as we go forward, studying the track record of the kingdom of God. The pattern goes like this: Christians pray. Jesus then pours out the Holy Spirit because Jesus is the By-My-Spirit King. The Holy Spirit brings a change of atmosphere; He destroys the influence of demonic power over a place, together with the hidden deceptions that are twisting life patterns into all the unloving distortions that the evil one engenders. When the Spirit comes, "He will convince the world of sin and righteousness and judgment" (John 16:8).

Soul Friendship: How They Made Disciples

The second reason was this. They possessed a method of disciple-making that we have completely forgotten today. It was what enabled the Irish Church to transform Irish society according to the commands of the King. That method was soul friendship.

Let me recommend, in passing, Ray Simpson's book *Soul Friendships: Celtic Insights into Spiritual Mentoring.*[93] His book sets forth the vision from the Celts, then gives instructions about how to build soul friendships today. He points out that "people in churches expend their energy on task-oriented programs which strain rather than enrich their relationships, and which deflect their attention from their own inner journey."[94] By contrast, the Celts anchored their experience of the kingdom in love relationships that were safe, pure, and Christ-centered, rather than in performance orientation and church activities.

This approach was rooted in the apostle John's relationship with Jesus. It was modeled out by Cassian in his friendship with Germanus. And it was recommended by Brigid, who gave the following advice to a young priest: Just as the water in a well is full of lime and good for nothing, so is a person without a soul friend. "Go off and don't eat until you get a soul friend."[95] Simpson quotes Aelred's treatise, *Spiritual Friendship.*

Friendship is nothing else but wisdom, and the person who abides in friendship abides in God, and God in them…He is entirely alone who is without a friend. But what happiness, what security, what joy to have someone to whom you dare to speak on terms of equality as to another self; one to whom you can unblushingly make known what progress you have made in the spiritual life; one to whom you can entrust all the secrets of your heart and before whom you can place all your plans.[96]

The soul friend becomes a safe and trustworthy older brother or sister, a listener, usually one who has already struggled with many of the issues of life guided by the word of God and the Holy Spirit.

In the Celtic church, people gained soul friends in a variety of ways. There was generally a willingness on the part of mature Christians to be on the lookout for people who needed a soul friend, and people who needed one were not afraid to ask. Since most Christians had grown up with a soul friend, they knew how to be one for someone else later in life. Many had multiple soul friendships, and they would last for years. Sometimes, the abbot of a house of prayer became the soul friend for new Christians, or sometimes he would appoint soul friends for people in his monastery or church. Usually (but not always), older men would be soul friends to younger men; older women to younger women. In this way, the Christian Church became, in every way, a family to new believers, who were loved and guided—and corrected when they needed correction.

It was this structure of soul friendships that separated the Celtic Church as a discipleship community from the Roman Church, which functioned as a religious institution. It is only as we comprehend this family structure that characterized the Celtic Church that we can then comprehend the success of the full-blown Celtic monasteries that were now emerging all over Ireland.

This became the underlying strength of a Church that successfully confronted demonic power to achieve a change of atmosphere from darkness to light over most or all of Celt country. Soul friendship in a milieu of a praying discipleship community was the hidden secret of successful spiritual warfare. Churches were communities that guarded the hearts of all of their members and surrounded them with love. Without this insight, we cannot understand the profound success of their efforts to advance the kingdom of God over the god of this world.

It is time for me to introduce you to the warrior monks.

19

The Warrior Monks: Columba

Bruce Ritchie, in his recent book, *Columba: The Faith of an Island Soldier*, has given us a full-blooded picture of spiritual conflict from the most famous monastic community of the Celts: Iona. For 500 years, the Gospel of the kingdom was drawing Christians into conflict with some very unsavory realities. Let me draw from Ritchie's book a picture of the shape of that conflict at the end of the sixth century but rooted in the first. Rooted, in fact, in the gift of kingdom keys that Jesus gave His disciples at a grotto known as The Gates of Hell.

Kingdom Keys

Pagan religion was a product of demonic power under the supervision of Satan. The kingdom of God was meant to overcome that power and set people free from it. It still is.

Matthew 16 tells the story of Jesus in Caesarea Philippi, a city that had quite a reputation in Jesus' day. Until recently, it had been called Paneas, after the Greek God, Pan. Jesus had brought his little band of disciples to one of the most infamous pagan worship centers in the middle east, a grotto called The Gates of Hell.[97] Here, for generations, people had been committing unspeakable acts with goats. The place was the haunt of demons who love to help people pervert sex. Jesus was

147

revealing to his little naive band of Jewish disciples that he was giving them authority to advance His kingdom against such powers as this. Even places like this one in Paneas would not be off-limits. Through His Church, He, the King, would set people free from satanic deception and bondage. This was the authority he was referring to as "the keys of the kingdom"— and the Gates of Hell would not prevail against it.

This was the version of the Gospel that the Irish, including Columba on the Isle of Iona, believed in and practiced, imitating both Antony and Evagrius, who believed the same Gospel. The keys were given to kingdom people to set people free "on earth as it is in heaven." For Columba and many of the Irish monks, the authority to liberate people from satanic power was a daily reality as they confronted paganism in Britain, and they were determined to advance the kingdom of God against it.

Here is how Bruce Ritchie summarizes the faith that grew up under Columba at Iona and at many other Irish monasteries—so different from the New Age ideas that prevail today in our post-modern world:

> ...Wherever missionary monks encountered non-Christian religion, the initial missional activity was not about persuading men and women intellectually. The first task was to engage demonic forces and destroy their authority. Non-Christian religion was an enemy. It was not a first building-block of spirituality, only needing redirection. Non-Christian religion was formed and inhabited by the demonic. It was not indwelt by God's Holy Spirit. It was to be put to flight.[98]

No Gospel progress could be made until Satanic pseudo-authority was broken. Any attempt to evangelize without first establishing the triumph of Christ over powers which held a particular locality in bondage, was fruitless exercise.[99]

The task of the missionary monk, through prayer and proclamation, was to break the rule of Satan over individuals and communities. Once that rule was broken, the Gospel could take root. ...The missionary monk brought the presence of the triumphant Christ, with His infinite conquering potential, into a situation.[100]

Each day was to be lived out as a soldier of Christ. Each day they battled on Christ's behalf against Satanic hordes of hell. Spiritual conflict dominated their faith horizon; and every phase of life, and every circumstance, was interpreted in relation to that warfare.[101]

Monastic communities, and the Church in general, had a job to do. They were supposed to advance the kingdom of God against a perverse, deceptive, dark, enslaving reality that had whole nations in its grip. And while the Church as a whole was to pursue God's kingdom and His righteousness, it was the mature monastic community that conducted an almost military vendetta against the gross evil of paganism. That was their job, and young men joined the Iona community with their eyes wide open to it.

Celtic War

These young men even looked the part. Banish forever from your imagination the picture of what a monk looks like. These monks did not shave their heads into tonsures, the way Roman monks were starting to do. The Irish looked more like the Nazirites of the Old Testament. They let their hair grow long, but then they shaved the front of their foreheads from ear to ear. These guys just looked fierce, more like lions than middle-aged, balding men.

Let me tell one of the many stories from Adamnan's *Life of Columba* to convey just how real the struggle was. Columba was traveling through the north, in Pict country, when he came upon a spring of water. The water here contained a malignancy, such that if people would dip their foot in it or drink it, they would break out in disease. This power was worshiped by pagans, and Druid priests had turned the spring into a worship center, not unlike the Gates of Hell in Caesarea Philippi.

Columba confronted this situation directly. Approaching the spring, he raised his hand, making the sign of the cross over the water and invoking the power of Jesus to transform the water into a healthful flow.[102] To him, the sign of the cross was an aggressive dislodging action, announcing the removal of a tenant who had abused the property. Now, the owner was back, and He was taking over. Columba, the owner's representative, was announcing the eviction order. After making decrees to this effect, Columba then entered the water and bathed in it to the glee of the Druids, who were sure that Columba had just sealed his own doom. But "from that day," writes Adamnan, "the demons departed from the spring; and not only was it not permitted to injure anyone but even, after the blessing of the saint and his washing therein, many diseases among the people were healed by the same spring."[103]

Adamnan's *Life of Columba* is chock full of stories like this.

A Parallel from Today

There is a tendency, in our day, to discount such stories. "Just legends," we say, feeling too high-minded to believe that these events actually happened.

But it may help us to connect with similar events recorded now in the twenty-first century, such as can be seen in George Otis's video, *An Unconventional War*.[104] Here, a band of Ugandan intercessors was called into battle against Joseph Koni, the leader of The Lord's Resistance Army, which had been terrorizing villages in northern Uganda, abducting young girls and forcing them into sexual slavery.[105]

The intercessors, through prayer, discovered that Koni's demonic power base was two springs of malignant water near the northern border of Uganda. They went to these springs, broke the power in the water, bathed in the springs, and claimed the victory of Christ. When the soldiers who went along with the intercessors saw this, they were instantly converted to Christ and were baptized.

Sometimes it helps to connect the stories of the past with contemporary events to counteract modern skepticism arising from a modern western worldview. For other present-day stories of spiritual conflict, I recommend two videos produced by Darren Wilson: "Father of Lights" and "Furious Love," both available from WP Films.[106]

The Island Soldier
Of all the "Twelve Apostles of Ireland," Columba became the most famous, with a reputation equal to that of Patrick himself. Consider the irony. Patrick was from "Scotland" (or, more properly, from Strathclyde) but brought the Gospel to Ireland because of King Niall's slave raid. A century later, Columba,

a descendant of Niall, is about to bring the slave-liberating Gospel back to "Scotland."

It is said that he is responsible for converting the Pictish people to Christ. However, Bruce Ritchie points out that there had been already a great many Celtic Christians ministering to their northern neighbors (remember Cadoc, for example), and the credit really belongs to the previous generation. However, there is no question but that the Iona prayer community had an enormous influence over Scotland. I believe that the prayers of Iona changed the atmosphere over Scotland and broke the power of darkness in the far north.

Columba's Story

Before the Iona years, Columba had already, by age forty-five, started some 300 praying churches in Ireland. This may seem like an exaggeration, but that is just how things were developing in sixth-century Ireland. Spiritual awakening was underway. And remember: the Irish were using a multiplication model of ministry, unlike us moderns, who start congregations and then try to add more and more people until we have a megachurch. By contrast, they would aim to bring people to maturity in Christ so that they would be capable of discipling others in other locales, who could disciple others, and so on. Small churches multiplying, according to Paul's advice in 2 Timothy 2:2: "And the things you have heard me say in the presence of many witnesses entrust to reliable men who will also be qualified to teach others."

All was going well with Columba until one day, he was seized with a desire to have a copy of a manuscript that his mentor, Finnian, had brought back from Whithorn.[107] He borrowed the manuscript and secretly copied it before returning it. When Finnian found out he had made a copy, he took offense, and Columba took offense at his offense, and the controversy exploded into an intertribal conflict—resulting in the infamous Battle of Cul Drebene, in which many people were killed. In the end, Columba was assigned an act of penance for his part in this conflict. He was banished from Ireland. So he boarded a curragh, a large version of the one-hide coracle, and with twelve prayer warriors, he sailed to Iona, just west of the Isle of Mull. There he and his monks built the most famous Celtic monastery of them all, a good example of how God takes a negative and turns it into a positive.

Iona was a part of the new extended kingdom of Dal Riata, which had recently spread over into what is today Argyll. These Irish immigrants were known as "Scoti," and it is they who would eventually give Scotland its name. So Iona, helping to promote and strengthen this immigration of people from Ireland, had a profound cultural impact, shaping Scotland into what it is today.

Iona was not an easy-going conviviality of Friar Tucks, making wine and welcoming tourists to their island retreat. Everything revolved around spiritual warfare, extending the kingdom of God into every nook and cranny of Scotland. At the center of the victory of Jesus was the reality of the Cross, as the apostle Paul had expressed:

> *When you were dead in your sins and in the uncircumcision of your sinful nature, God made you alive with Christ. He forgave us all our sins, having canceled the written code, with its regulations, that was against us and that stood opposed to us; he took it away nailing it to the cross. And*

having disarmed the powers and authorities, he made a
public spectacle of them, triumphing over them by the cross.

Colossians 2:13-15

This cross-victory was now being pressed out to the farthest western extremity of the human race. Beginning with Patrick, the Irish were aware that God had given them responsibility to extend that Cross-victory as far west as it would go, even out into the Atlantic Ocean. (See the next chapter, which describes another of the Twelve Apostles of Ireland.)

When Columba made the sign of the cross in the face of his Druid adversaries, it was an aggressive announcement that the kingdom of love and freedom was now replacing the bondage and perverse legalism of the pagan system. And when they carved huge eight-to-twenty-foot Celtic crosses and set them up throughout the countryside, and at the center of their monasteries, it was a statement about the triumph of Christ over the kingdom of darkness. They were taking back God's Creation and helping King Jesus to "restore all things."

The Cross in the Middle of It All

As you might expect, community prayer life also revolved around the triumph of the Cross. The most important community prayer gatherings were at 9 a.m., at noon, and at 3 p.m., and each of these meetings revolved around the Cross. The first of these commemorated the moment Jesus was crucified. In addition, the outpouring of the Holy Spirit on Pentecost Day happened "at the third hour" (9 a.m.).

The sixth hour (noon) commemorated the moment of the day Jesus died when supernatural darkness covered the land. As far as the monks were concerned, this was the moment when the actual confrontation of satanic power had taken place in the heavenly realms.

The ninth hour (3 p.m.) was the moment Jesus breathed His last, and the victory was complete. The ninth hour was also the hour when John and Peter went to the temple afterward, and the power of the Holy Spirit began to flow from the Gate Beautiful out to the nations for healing and deliverance (Acts 3:1).

So monastic communities were tying their prayer life to the victory of the Cross, which had the power to change the world. Everything was to flow from that victory. It was the anchor for every ship, the grocer for every meal. This was the meaning behind what would evolve into the Canonical Hours of all monastic communities through the Middle Ages. Other community prayer times would be added throughout the day and night, but, as Bruce Ritchie describes, the daily prayer schedule was always anchored to these three mid-day gatherings that honed in on the victory of Jesus that changed the world. And as the prayer movement evolved into a full-fledged monastic movement, a more or less consistent pattern, still open to change, emerged among the Irish.

But the Irish never put God in a box. And, at any rate, God refused to be put in a box. As we shall see in the next chapter.

20

BRENDAN THE NAVIGATOR

The Twelve Apostles of Ireland completed the transformation of Ireland once and for all. With Generation Five, the old gods were finished by the time these warrior monks were done with them. That is why the monasteries of the warriors became so popular. They attracted thousands of young men to their strict devotion. Yes, they were austere. Army life was not fun. But they wanted to be on the winning side.[108]

The warrior monks were a rare breed: pursuing holiness as though it were going out of style; confronting barbaric gods who, for the first time in history, had to back down; building an army of prayer warriors out of sometimes very poor raw material. They were a generation that had a good start on changing the world. This new generation of prayer warriors had found out that life under the King of kings has a new definition: faith, hope, and love. They had enough of these commodities to believe that Ireland could be different from what they had grown up with. They believed in the goodness of the Man on the Cross, and now a massive force, the Spirit of God, was working hand-in-glove with them to complete the change.

And then, God led them beyond Ireland, beyond, even, the kingdom of Dal Riata. It was a big world out there, and the next generation began to look to new horizons. The fifth generation became a missionary generation.

Brendan the Navigator

Brendan was one of the "apostles of Ireland" who, like Columba, graduated from Finnian's school. He also grew up under the mentoring of Ita, a woman of great saintliness (the generation after Brigid.) This shows us that sometimes young men were discipled by "mothers" rather than "fathers" in Christ. After graduating from Finnian's school, he began founding praying churches. He is best known for the full-fledged monastery he founded at Clonfert, which kept spinning off more praying churches.

One day, he took a spiritual retreat to the southwestern tip of Ireland, near where he had grown up as a boy. His retreat overlooked the Atlantic Ocean. There, he was filled with the conviction that God was calling him to launch himself into a great journey in search of "the Isle of Promise." It was as though a piece of heaven were awaiting him across the waters, and he was to go looking until he found it. He wrote a poem about this very personal vision that had come into his life. The poem captures the sense of journey embedded in Celtic Christianity—and the risk implied in all true steps of faith:

Shall I abandon, O King of Mysteries, the soft comforts of home? Shall I turn my back on my native land, and my face towards the sea?

Shall I put myself wholly at the mercy of God, without silver, without a horse, without fame and honour? Shall I throw myself wholly on the King of kings, without sword and shield, without food and drink, without a bed to lie on?

Shall I say farewell to my beautiful land, placing myself under Christ's yoke? Shall I pour out my heart to him, confessing my manifold sins and begging forgiveness, tears streaming down my cheeks?

Shall I leave the prints of my knees on the sandy beach, a record of my final prayer in my native land? Shall I then suffer every kind of wound that the sea can inflict?

Shall I take my tiny coracle across the wide sparkling ocean? O King of the Glorious Heaven, shall I go of my own choice upon the sea?

O Christ, will you help me on the wild waves?[109]

Brendan spent the next weeks making a large coracle (or curragh), a vessel of wattle (sticks), and ox hides tanned with oak bark, like the one Patrick had assigned to MacCuill Greccae, only far larger and more seaworthy. Then, together with fourteen monks and perhaps two or three others who wanted to come along for the sheer adventure of it, they embarked on their search for the Isle of Promise.

The True Significance of the Voyage

No one today knows where they went on their voyage, which seems to have taken them well over a year to complete. But some believe that Brendan got as far as Newfoundland, then returned to Ireland by way of the Azores. And there is some evidence for this: First, the document that has come down to us, "The Voyage of St. Brendan," does describe an iceberg. So you have to ask, how could he have described an iceberg if he hadn't actually seen one—there are no icebergs anywhere near Ireland and never have been. Second, Native Americans have a type of craft they learned to build called a "bull boat," remarkably similar to an Irish coracle. Could they have obtained their design directly from early Irish visitors? Third, an Irishman named Tim Severin in 1978 built a coracle like the one Brendan would have used and actually did cross the Atlantic Ocean, just to prove that it could be done. (Tim told his story in the 1978 film, "The Brendan Voyage.") So it is possible that Brendan did actually make it all the way across the Atlantic Ocean in the 6th century!

But in my judgment, the importance of the voyage of Brendan the Navigator lies elsewhere. The tale of his voyage was developed into an Irish *immram*—a Celtic odyssey or saga. This saga, published as "The Voyage of St. Brendan," sparked the imagination of the entire European continent. It makes no claims at being historical; clearly, it was developed into a tale, designed to be told around a campfire, full of lessons for Christians. But it had an amazingly deep and broad impact well beyond Ireland. It was translated into several languages; over a hundred medieval manuscripts of it still exist to this day in various languages. And with each translation, the tale changed little by little.

So, while we don't know where Brendan went on his voyage, we have a very good idea of where *the story* of his voyage went. It went everywhere! And it sparked an idea among Europeans: that God had a Promised Land across the ocean to the west, just beckoning to Europeans to come and discover it. Brendan's "Isle of Promise" morphed into a Promised Land across the ocean, which surely had an impact on Christians nine hundred years later, who actually did go searching for that Promised Land across the ocean.

Power-and-Might churches would get a hold of that vision, it is true, and the results would be, at best, mixed. But the original seed was a Holy Spirit seed, nurtured in the life of a very devoted follower of Jesus, a man of great humility and love, who went on a search for the kingdom of God on earth as it is in heaven.

The humility and goodness of this man are confirmed by my last story of Brendan. By the end of his life, in 577 AD, he began to see how people were idolizing the saints of the past, almost worshiping them, and preserving their relics (bones), even buying and selling relics. Returning late in life from trips to Wales and Iona, and knowing that his death was approaching, he made arrangements to have his body returned to Clonfert in a luggage cart—disguised as baggage, then secretly buried where it would not be found.

I believe that most of the Celtic saints would not have approved of the trafficking in relics (their relics!) that became so common in later years. Nor would they have approved of the way their stories would be bandied about as great miracle workers by later generations of "miracle hunters." Nor would they have approved of the practice of praying to saints, rather than to Christ—nor of any practice whatever of glorifying themselves. The men and women of the ancient Celtic Church were men and women of genuine humility. "Just put my body in the ground and leave my bones alone!" By and large, that was their very humble attitude.

21

COMGALL AND THE 24/7 PRAYER MOVEMENT

The early houses of prayer had as their goal to help people "pray without ceasing." But then another idea came into being, as it has today: to develop communities for day-and-night prayer and worship. In a community like that, every member is organized into teams to provide God with worship and prayer in shifts so that the flame on the altar never goes out, day or night. How did this idea get started?

Laus Perennis—Perpetual Praise

Back in the days before Constantine, there was a Roman legion called the Theban Legion, on a tour of duty in the Swiss Alps, in one of the most beautiful mountain valleys on God's green earth. The co-Emperors Diocletian and Maxentius were furious persecutors of Christians, and the order went out to the legions that every soldier in the Roman army needed to worship Maxentius. Anyone who refused would be killed. The Theban Legion had become entirely Christian, and so this order created an impossible decision for them.

The head of the legion, Maurice, himself a Christian, put the decision before his men. Maxentius, who apparently was there to personally enforce the decision (and seeing that none were going to worship him), decreed that the legion should be decimated. Which meant this: They would start with a tenth of the legion, chosen by lot, and kill them. Then they would give the other nine-tenths the opportunity to get started worshiping the Emperor. Then, if they still refused, they would choose another tenth and kill them; if that didn't change some minds, they would keep going until every legionnaire was *decimated*. In the end, not a single one worshiped Maxentius; all remained faithful to Jesus as a witness to the King, and their bodies were dumped in a mass grave and buried there in that Alpine valley.

One hundred and fifty years later, the mass grave was rediscovered, and Bishop Eucherius of Tours published the story about who these men were and how they got there. At that time, the King of Burgundy, a Frankish king named Sigismund (whose kingdom now included that mountain valley), became a Christian. Upon hearing of the Theban Legion, he built a monastery at the mass grave in honor of Maurice and his legion. In establishing the monastery, though, he drew upon the traditions of the East—specifically "The Sleepless Ones," a monastic order in Constantinople initiated by the archimandrite Alexander.

So it was the Franks who built the first Western 24/7 prayer community, right there in that Alpine valley. Significantly, from then on (522 AD), the Frankish kingdom began to grow to the West until it overtook the ancient Roman province of Gaul and eventually became France. And as the Frankish kingdom grew, so did the Frankish monasteries. Eventually, the Celtic and Frankish prayer communities would send representatives to each other's communities to encourage one another in prayer.

Irish Perpetual Harmonies

Somehow, we don't know exactly how, this movement spread to Ireland. There is a document called "The Welsh Triads," which lists three 24/7 "Perpetual Harmonies" in Celt country:[110]

> *Three Perpetual Harmonies of the Island of Britain*
> *One was at the Island of Afallach*
> *and the second at Caer Garadawg,*
> *and the third at Bangor.*[111]

Norma Lorre Goodrich, a specialist in ancient Welsh documents and place names, has identified these names. In addition to Bangor, Ireland, there was a "perpetual harmony" on the Isle of Man (Afallach) and at Holyrood (Edinburgh—Caer Garadawg). If this is accurate, then, by the sixth century, each of the land masses of Britain had something in the nature of 2400 monks singing perpetual praises to God in one-hour shifts. This, in other words, could have been a part of the spiritual warfare that transformed Europe out of paganism by changing the atmosphere over the nations. Here's the idea: Worship draws down the presence of God and invites "times of refreshing from the presence of the Lord." God inhabits the praises of His people.

Comgall

Comgall, a close friend of Columba and a graduate of Finnian's school, was entrusted with building the perpetual harmony in Ireland—at Bangor, on the south shore of Belfast Lough opposite Carrickfergus. Comgall was an unlikely choice for God to put in charge of musicians. His background? He was a Pictish warrior and the son of a warrior. One thing about the

Picts: they excelled in the use of tattoos, especially the warriors. It was the tattoos that caused the Romans to call them Picts—because of the pictures on their skin. So imagine Comgall, a heavily tattooed man, perhaps with red hair, his head shaved above the forehead from ear to ear, and the rest of his hair flowing out behind to the shoulders. You would not want to meet this man in a dark alley at night. If anyone understood the principle of worship as *warfare*, it was Comgall.

In principle, there were twenty-four teams of 100 monks each, singing praise to God around the clock. At its height, however, there were a great many more than 2400 men who signed up for this privilege at Bangor—there were 8000, making this monastery the most flourishing and successful of all the Irish monasteries.

And yet, it was also the most austere and disciplined of them all. These were the Green Berets of Irish monasticism. If you were going to have the honor of joining one of these teams, you had to deal with sin in your life, and they were going to help you do it through assigned penances. Looked at one way—these penances were punishments for sin. Looked at another—they were restoratives. They helped a person claw his way back from hurts caused by sin so that relationships could be restored. Most monasteries had a list of "penitentials," prescribed "remedies for the wounds according to the rulings of the fathers before us," as one penitential put it.[112]

These rules were always, it seems, based on the eight deadly thoughts of Evagrius and Cassian. Behind them was the awareness that sin wounds people; it hurts the fabric of love growing up in a community, and it can interfere with free communication between ourselves and God, so important in a community like Bangor. People who allow sin in their lives can still offer praise to God, but it ends up being lip service if sin continues to be tolerated. And part of the purpose of the penances (often assigned fasts or acts of restitution) was to discourage sin by making it painful to the person who commits sin, more than to the victim who may have been wronged. (In our culture, we assign prison terms to criminals until they have paid their "debt to society," but we ignore the whole issue of restoring the relationships that have been broken because of sin.)

Dying To Self
Even besides the penances, life at Bangor was hard. Sometimes, meals consisted of nothing but bread and water with herbs. Only one full meal was permitted per day, in the evening. (Hopefully, that was not the meal of bread, water, and herbs!) Monks who signed up for their tour of duty at Bangor knew what they were getting into, and, amazingly, they were up for it.

Their own austerity did not mean that they did not believe in treating others to richer fare. At one point, there was a shortage of food. Comgall was concerned because guests were to arrive that evening, and they wanted to treat them hospitably. So he prayed for provision, and God brought a school of fish close to the monastery, so there would be plenty of food—for the guests!

Comgall was known to have taken several trips to Scotland to visit his friend, Columba. They took several mission trips together among the Picts, and perhaps this is how a 24/7 prayer community was formed in Scotland. Of course, Comgall would have helped bridge the cultural gap between himself and the Picts. (Alas, Columba had no tattoos.)

Let me say a final word about austerity because severity to the body was a major part of Celtic spirituality, especially at Bangor. They borrowed that from the Desert Fathers.

Comgall's very first attempt at establishing a monastery had been a disaster because it was so austere. He built a monastery in Lough Erne. But in the winter, life was so harsh that seven of the prayer warriors perished from hunger and cold. This had to have been felt as a disaster; it cannot have been how Comgall had foreseen things to end for them. I wonder if this wasn't a parallel to Antony's first experience challenging the demons in the graveyard, which ended in disaster. It does seem to me that those who are called with high callings are sometimes allowed to walk through deep struggles and defeats before being entrusted with high authority in God's kingdom. This is how I interpret Comgall's first disaster. But Comgall kept going, establishing one of the most flourishing houses of prayer in Ireland—surely the most famous of them all, besides Iona.

On the other hand, he, like Evagrius before him, met with an untimely and painful end because of physical problems directly caused by that severe lifestyle. This seems a tragedy to me. While it is not for me to question these great leaders of the past, it does seem worth pointing out one verse in Colossians that would have challenged the extreme fasting (extremism that Cassian, remember, had begun to question after his experiences in the desert):

> *Therefore, if you died with Christ from the basic principles of the world, why, as though living in the world, do you subject yourselves to regulations—"Do not touch, do not taste, do not handle," which all concern things which perish with the using—*

according to the commandments and doctrines of men? These things indeed have an appearance of wisdom in self-imposed religion, false humility, and neglect of the body, but are of no value against the indulgence of the flesh.

Colossians 2:20-23

It seems to me that this verse from the apostle Paul could have been a corrective that would have extended these men's lives considerably, and saved them a painful death. Both Evagrius and Comgall were flames that burned very, very bright; but the flame went out too soon, to everybody's loss.

22

BENEDICT AND GREGORY

In the year 597, the year that Columba died, something happened that was to drastically change everything in Britain. Pope Gregory the Great sent his bishop, a Benedictine monk named Augustine (not to be confused with Augustine of Hippo two centuries before), to begin an evangelistic outreach to the Anglo-Saxons in England. The Roman Church was returning to Britain after a two-hundred-year absence.

To understand this event, let me take you back to Rome. The fifth century had not been kind to this city, which had fallen into the hands of the Goths. Gone were the days of cushy splendor and worldly power for the Christians. During these years, the Romans learned to pray, and there grew many houses of prayer, just as we have seen among the Celts. During the height of this interest in prayer, there rose up a champion of prayer, Benedict of Nursia, who, around the turn of the century, renounced his education in Rome to live as a hermit in a cave east of Rome. The cave was located in a beautiful valley of deep shadows at Subiaco, and in time, this became Benedict's first monastery. Around 530, Benedict moved from there to found the monastery at Monte Cassino further south, where he developed the Rule of St. Benedict, surely the most influential single document in the history of monastic movements.

During the next generation, Rome passed through a particularly gruesome period full of wars and plagues. During the sixth century, there rose up one of the most famous and influential popes—Gregory the Great, who wrote *The Life of St. Benedict* as part of a larger body of writings that are preserved to this day.[113] Benedict had died while Gregory was still a small child, but he was able to garner stories of his life from those who had known him.

Totila and Benedict

One story from the *Life of St. Benedict* will serve to demonstrate the power of the Spirit-filled life that these early saints were known for. The story will also show the similarity to Celtic saints like Patrick, Brigid, Columba, and Comgall, all of whom gained their inspiration from the same sources: John Cassian and Martin of Tours.

The following event happened at the end of Benedict's life, when he was visited by Totila, King of the Ostrogoths, in 542. Totila had heard of Benedict and the gift of prophecy that flowed as a result of his prayer life. He decided to test the saint, so he dressed up one of his men, Riggo, as himself. Then he sent Riggo with a large and impressive retinue into the Monte Cassino monastery to see if he could fool the Christian leader. Benedict, immediately spotting the ruse, shouted at Riggo, "Take off those clothes; they do not belong to you!"

Foiled in their ruse and awed by Benedict's prophetic gift (actually, a word of knowledge), the whole group of pagans prostrated themselves before Benedict, and Totila came forward to ask forgiveness. Whereupon Benedict spoke the following prophecy: "You are doing much evil, and you have done much evil. It is time to stop this bad behavior! At any rate, you will enter Rome, you will cross the sea. You will reign nine years and die on the tenth."[114]

Gregory says that Totila was a nicer man after that, but I fail to see any evidence for this. In 546, he completely depopulated Rome, doing to it what the Romans had done to Jerusalem under Hadrian. Rome became a ghost town. The Byzantines later recaptured Rome, but then Totila recaptured it again, inviting people to repopulate the city—then the Byzantines, back again under Justinian in 552. At which point, the Goths lost control of the city, and Totila died in the very year that Benedict had prophesied.

On top of all this instability, there came a great plague, the Plague of Justinian, that afflicted the entire remains of the Roman empire, radiating now from Constantinople (Byzantium) beginning 541. Over 25 million died in this plague, which continued on and off for two centuries.

Gregory the Great and the Prayer Movement

This man we know as Gregory the Great grew up and became Prefect of Rome during this difficult time. But it is during seasons of difficulty that people feel most sharply their need for God—and that was certainly true of Rome during the sixth century. Gregory turned his villa into a monastery and, apparently, was among the first to try out The Rule of St. Benedict at his "St. Andrew's monastery." After Benedict became Pope, a man named Augustine became prior to that monastery. This is the man Gregory would send to England to become the first Archbishop of Canterbury.

Benedict and Gregory! These two men are to be regarded as perhaps the best of the Roman Church. (John Calvin, 1000 years later, called Pope Gregory "the last good pope.") Benedict, drawing together the influences of Martin of Tours and John Cassian, developed his "Rule" for monasteries that was to have such positive practical and inspirational effect that it still serves monastic communities to this day. During future seasons of decline, future generations of Roman Catholic monks (i.e., the Cistercians of the 11th and 12th centuries) would look to their Benedictine roots and draw the goodness from those roots.

And yet.

When Gregory sent Augustine to England to win the Anglo-Saxons for Christ, something went terribly wrong. These newcomers now joining together with the Celts had so very much in common with them, and yet, try as they might, they could not come into agreement. Why not? That is the question to be explored in the next chapter.

23

A Dagger of Divisiveness

It is Bede, a Benedictine monk writing 130 years later, who tells the story. Bede treats Augustine's arrival as though it were the advent, at long last, of real Christianity. "The blessed Pope Gregory...transformed our still idolatrous nation into a church of Christ." From Bede's point of view, Gregory deserves the title "Apostle to the English."[115]

Bede then launches into the story of Augustine's initial encounter with the Celts, who had established their Christian presence on the island two centuries before—but not yet among Anglo-Saxons. Augustine, he says, was eager for a united Christian presence with the Celts. But, in Bede's words,

> ...despite protracted discussions, neither the prayers nor the advice nor the censures of Augustine and his companions could obtain the compliance of the Britons, who stubbornly preferred their own customs to those in universal use among Christian Churches.[116]

As the story goes, Augustine then said, "Let's see what God will say about this matter"—and he produced a blind man, inviting the Celts to pray for him. They did this, but the man was not healed. Then Augustine prayed for him—and he was healed, thus proving whose side God is taking, now that Rome has entered the scene. The Britons, however, were all the more "stubborn" and asked for another conference at a later date, after consulting with their people, whether or not they should submit to Augustine's authority.

In the intervening weeks, the Celts consulted with a certain hermit whom they regarded as the wisest man in the land. This hermit had spent his life avoiding the limelight, and so to this day, we do not even know his name. This paragon of humility told them to accept Augustine on one condition: that he shall prove his humility. If he appears humble to them, then, by all means, they should submit to him, he said. But if not, then they should not submit to or accept him. Particularly, he said, look for this sign: If he rises when you arrive in his presence, that is a sign that he is honoring you; it is the most important sign of humility that you are to look for.

That Fateful Meeting

Seven Celtic bishops showed up in the next conference, and when they arrived, Augustine did not rise to greet them, nor did he show any humility whatsoever. On the contrary, he made three demands of them: "to keep Easter at the correct time; to complete the Sacrament of Baptism...according to the rites of the holy, Roman, and apostolic Church; and to join with us in preaching the word of God to the English."[117] These are the tests that Augustine had decided to put on the Britons (Celts). Unfortunately, he didn't realize that they were putting him to their own test as well—and that he had already flunked!

To Bede, who is telling the story, this is just further evidence of the stubbornness of the Celts. So then Augustine, according to Bede, made a well-deserved threat "that was also a prophecy. If they refused to accept peace with their fellow Christians, then they must accept war with their enemies." Bede goes on to describe a horrible event that took place at a later date, a battle during which the warrior monks of Bangor assembled by the hundreds to pray and fast for a Celtic victory against the Saxon king Ethelfrid. Not only did the Celts lose the battle, but the monks were destroyed in large numbers, once again paying the penalty for their "stubbornness."

Why do I find Bede's story so disturbing? Perhaps it is because Bede presents a picture of God that is so different from the God I have come to know. Here is a God who plays favorites among Christians and who uses miracles to prove who He likes better. He is a God who curses faithful Christians because they are not observing Easter on "the proper day" and slaughters them out of righteous indignation. He is a God who destroys the Christian unity that had been enjoyed pretty well everywhere up to this point in Britain because this unity is not as important as other religious issues that allegedly take precedence in the heart of God. The scriptural formula for preserving unity (Philippians 2, Ephesians 4) is exactly what the Celtic hermit was wisely recommending. Yet Bede presents this way as a silly attempt on the part of the Celts to avoid submitting to The One True Religion.

As we examine this story carefully, Augustine was not actually seeking unity; he was seeking submission. To his mind, the price of unity was uniformity, that is, conformity to the Roman way, which Bede mistakes as a search for unity. But unity and uniformity are not the same thing.

Behind this dagger of disunity that has been thrust into the breach between Romans and Celts, there are deeper issues that are just now starting to show. The spiritual stronghold of Power-and-Might Christianity has seemed innocuous enough at the beginning of its intrusion into the Church during the fourth century. During those early years, it will replace, by degrees, the original "By-My-Spirit" mindset, the original paradigm, with its seven ingredients, that Jesus had given to His disciples at the beginning, confirmed on the Day of Pentecost. The Celts are still operating by those kingdom principles, taught by the King, dealing with humility and the human heart in reliance on the Spirit of God.

Augustine, on the other hand, is reflecting a dramatic change that has happened in Rome during the intervening two centuries: The Roman Church has turned itself into a religious institution, remarkably similar to the Sadduceean system that Jesus had confronted in the Temple. And the criteria Augustine is using to evaluate all Christians are the religious ones Rome has decided are necessary for all Christians to agree on. These religious issues are not going to go away.

Religion? Or Discipleship Community?

What is entering from Rome is a *religious institution*. This concept, this paradigm, seems right to them, and it is astonishing to Augustine that the Celts cannot accept this change from a discipleship community into a religion. But the whole concept of "the one true religion" under control of a hierarchy of archbishops is foreign to them. It seems foreign because it *is* foreign. For centuries, they have been content to make disciples, according to the original command of Christ. Jesus Christ is the everlasting Father (Isaiah 9:6), who represents the Father to all people everywhere. Jesus is the only papa they need. Their mindset, their paradigm is a kingdom paradigm, not a religious one.

The difference between these two ways of being Christian is going to grow wider and wider. And the issues are not as trivial as they might at first seem.

As we shall see.

Iona

Lindisfarne

Bernicia

STRATHCLYDE

Whitby

NORTHUMBRIA

Deira

MERCIA

EAST
ANGLIA

WALES

ESSEX

Canterbury

WESSEX

KENT

CORNWALL

SUSSEX

THE SEVENTH-CENTURY
ANGLO-SAXON WORLD

24

OSWALD AND AIDAN, GENERATION SIX

It is time for us to look at the Anglo-Saxons, who, during the fifth and sixth centuries, had been securing their hold on England and, at the same time, dividing themselves into warring kingdoms. By the 7th century, you had Bernicia in the north, then Deira (south to York). These two together comprised the region of Northumbria. The center of England was occupied by Mercia. Four kingdoms occupied the southeast corner of England: East Anglia, Essex, Kent, and Sussex. Southwest England became Wessex ("West Saxons"). (See map.)

The Celts (called "Britons") still occupied Wales (but not yet called Wales), Strathclyde (which now included the Lake District in the north), and Cornwall in the southwest corner. Since the death of Arthur (assuming he was a historical person), the Anglo-Saxons had spread further and further west, absorbing more and more territory. The western boundary of the Anglo–Saxon kingdoms was, therefore, quite fluid by that time.

The Roman Approach

In the wake of Augustine's arrival in Kent (at Canterbury, southeast corner), Rome is now attempting to convert these people to Christ. Their preferred approach is to form alliances with kings, whom they convert to Christianity so that they will participate in the religion and the sacraments of the Church. This is what will make nations "Christian." They want the king to join the Church and participate in the sacraments. Then, the people are baptized, and the nation is considered Christian. From the top down.

But this is a risky approach. It depends on the faithfulness of kings, who prove to be quite fickle, and who have a way of merely using the Church to get power and prestige. But, for better or for worse, this is how it went:

The King of East Anglia decided to go to war against Aethelfrith in the far north. He killed Aethelfrith, installing his king, Edwin, as king of Northumbria (Deira and Bernicia, combined.) Aethelfrith's sons fled to Dalriata (Scotland) in the north, where they came under the influence of Columba's Iona network of communities. Columba had died the same year Augustine had arrived, so now there was a succession of Abbotts leading not just a single monastery but dozens of prayer communities all over Scotland.

Meanwhile, Edwin decided to form a marital alliance with Kent and brought up Aethelburg, sister of the Kentish king, to be his queen. This woman had become a Christian under Roman and Frankish influence. The Catholic bishop, Paulinus, who was to become the first Archbishop of York, accompanied her to York to begin converting Northumbrians to Christ. He found a few Celtic Christians there and sent them packing. Then he built a handsome stone basilica in York, the type of building that would impress kings. Eventually convincing King Edwin to become a Christian, he held a baptismal service, and thousands of people were baptized at York. These people were not discipled; the idea was to get them participating in the sacraments, regardless of whether or not they actually followed Jesus as King. Again, this top-down approach to evangelism is typical of Power-and-Might Christianity.

Unfortunately, the story did not end there. Penda, king of Mercia, formed an alliance with Edwin's foster-brother Cadwallon to defeat Edwin at the Battle of Hatfield Chase in 632. Edwin was slain. The battle was a bloody one. Bishop Paulinus left York for safety in the south, never to return. Most of the people he had baptized now returned to paganism, reasoning that the Christians' God "doesn't seem to be much good."

Ray Simpson describes the carnage that followed, a scene often repeated among the Anglo-Saxons and their warring kingdoms: "Cadwallon…inflicted unspeakable atrocities upon those fractious, shepherdless people. Their kingdoms became killing fields. They were a sea of blood. …Was there nothing left to these Northumbrians other than treachery and rule by terror?[118]

The By-My-Spirit Alternative

But the children of the slain King Aethelfrith, forced into Scottish exile by the violence of the times, discovered an answer that is well portrayed in Ray Simpson's lightly fictionalized biography, *Aidan of Lindisfarne: Irish Flame Warms a New World*. Oswald, the eldest son of the slain King Aethelfrith, became deeply impressed with the villages of God that Iona had planted in Dalriata (Scotland). Thoroughly converted to Christ, after several years, Oswald decided to return to Bernicia to try to reclaim the throne that was rightfully his. He recruited a small army of Northumbrians and Irish soldiers and challenged Cadwallon at a place on Hadrian's wall called Arthur's Fort, which became known as Birdoswald.

On the night before the battle, Oswald had a dream. In it, there appeared a gigantic image of Columba, who was speaking to him and his men, quoting from the Book of Joshua: "'Be strong and of good courage, for I will be with you.'" Columba continued: "March out tomorrow, your foes will be put to flight, Cadwallon will be slain, and you will return in triumph, for this is a just cause."[119] During his life, Columba had spoken dozens, if not hundreds of prophecies. Apparently, even in death, he was still doing this!

The following day, Oswald told his men about the dream. Though his forces were dwarfed by the greater army of his foe, Oswald defeated them, Cadwallon was slain, and the Anglo-Saxon soldiers were converted to Christ when they saw the fulfillment of the prophetic dream. Oswald thus began to rule Northumbria (Deira and Bernicia) from his capital at Bamburgh castle. Without delay, he sent word to Iona, asking for Irish missionaries to minister the Gospel of the kingdom to his Anglo-Saxon countrymen.

Iona Sends Missionaries
Recognizing the opportunity of a lifetime, the Iona community selected their most scholarly and experienced monk, Corman, to answer the call.

Within the year, however, Corman was back, complaining of the stubbornness of the Anglo-Saxons and telling story after story of his failure to get through to them. He had done his best but had failed miserably.

Whereupon a young monk, Aidan, stood up and spoke his mind to Corman, "My brother, it seems to me you have been unreasonably harsh upon your ignorant hearers. I think you gave them the meat of God's Word; perhaps with hindsight, it would have been better to have fed them with the milk until, little by little, as they grew strong on the food of God's Word, they became capable of carrying out spiritual disciplines. You were zealous to lay upon them our spiritual practices. Perhaps it would have been better to let their own practices grow out of their newly found love of God, even if they seemed strange to us."[120]

As a reward for this bold speech, Aidan was instantly selected to be Corman's replacement! He selected a team of twelve to accompany him, and off they went to take up the challenge that few other Celtic Christians had managed to undertake: introducing the kingdom of God to warlike, pagan Anglo-Saxons who had been making enemies right and left.

Aidan and Oswald Together

Soon after the team showed up in Northumbria, Oswald held a banquet to welcome the new arrivals. To express his commitment to Aidan, during the height of the festivities, he presented the monk with a valuable war horse, saying that this prized animal would enable Aidan to travel to the farthest corners of his kingdom to present the Gospel.

But this gesture took Aidan by surprise. It didn't fit in with his plans or his lifestyle as a (Celtic) Christian. So Aidan, in return, did the unthinkable. He stood up in the assembly and explained that if he accepted the horse, it would separate him from all the people he was charged with bringing to Christ—because they did not have the means to afford a warhorse—or any horse at all. It was Aidan's intention, wherever possible, to walk everywhere, to be a pedestrian!

This is what he said, and this is exactly what he did for the rest of his life. And everywhere he walked, he would greet people, ask them if they knew Jesus, and tell them about the King of Nations. But in explaining this lifestyle decision to Oswald and rejecting that gift in front of that crowd, he was taking a terrible risk—to lose the favor of the King before they had even had a chance to build a friendship.

That night, King Oswald learned a lesson in humility from a follower of the humble King, Jesus. He might have been offended, but he had already learned from the monks of Iona how to place all offenses on the cross. His friendship with Aidan came through that test stronger than ever. It clarified how things stood between the two of them: they were equals under the domain of King Jesus. Both needed to learn humility from the real King of Northumbria.

Whereas Paulinus had built a basilica for religious services, Aidan still followed the original vision of the Church—to make disciples. So he started his ministry not by building a cathedral but by starting a school for boys. And, while Oswald would have given him virtually any locale for his school and headquarters, Aidan chose a remote island, separated from the mainland by a causeway that was covered by sea-water much of the time: the Holy Isle of Lindisfarne, just north of the royal center of Bamburgh where King Oswald lived. This would be the location not only of Aidan's school but of the village of God that Celtic Christians built to live out the pattern of kingdom living. This would become the true evangelistic center from which most of Anglo-Saxon country would come to Jesus.

At the start, they built a wooden chapel, a set of accommodations for monks, another for schoolboys, a dining hall, guest facilities, and a scriptorium for the production of manuscripts. Then: a hospital, a kiln, storehouses, a smithy, and a boatbuilders' workshop. Bede tells us that, even though Oswald offered to endow whatever buildings Aidan might have desired, the team chose to live simply. Their goal was not to impress kings with a splendid religion but to walk out the loving lifestyle of Jesus, taught in the gospels that graced their new chapel and which they copied furiously, to get the Word out. The Word, still hand-lettered on vellum, was the anchor for every new village of God they would establish.

Though Aidan had been made a full-fledged bishop, he chose, as Martin of Tours had done two centuries before, to present himself as a simple man, easily accessed and readily available to the poor. What money he did receive from Oswald, he often used to purchase the freedom of slaves, for the Celtic church had been opposing slavery since the days of Patrick. His school attracted a wide variety of Anglo-Saxons—some ex-slaves and some the children of kings. At school, they all learned that God does not play favorites. Many Anglo-Saxons were impressed with this new picture of God and the treatment they received from His representatives.

Aidan was well received by everyone at the royal centers of Northumbria. As the years passed, the Christian faith was warmly embraced, not just because King Oswald embraced it but because the people themselves were learning of and embracing the King of Kings.

What a contrast this faith from the north was, when laid against the other making its way up from the kingdom of Kent in the south, for the Celts remembered the word of the apostle James, brother to Jesus:

> *If you show special attention to the man wearing fine clothes and say, "Here's a good seat for you," but say to the poor man, "You stand there" or "Sit on the floor by my feet," have you not discriminated among yourselves and become judges with evil thoughts?*
>
> *James 2:3–4*

The Celts did not spread the faith by going after kings. Bruce Ritchie explains this in his book about Columba and the Iona community:

> *Other missions, more closely aligned to State interests, understood conversion differently. Some saw mission in terms of a cultural Christianization of communities, in which individual faith of the heart was of minor importance. They worked on the assumption that Christian beliefs would follow cultural Christianisation. But (Columba's) evangelical missions saw it in reverse. For them, individuals had to come to a personal faith of the heart before groups of converts could then become the building blocks of a Christian society. …There was an awareness that the mission of Christ and the apostles did not include the conversion of kings.*[121]

The Provision of Oswald

At first, of course, it was King Oswald who opened the door for the Gospel throughout England. Oswald was one of the most extraordinary kings England ever had. Such favor was upon him that he quickly spread the influence of Christ throughout most of Britain. Bede writes:

> ...At length he brought under his scepter all the peoples and provinces of Britain speaking the four languages, British, Pictish, Irish, and English.
>
> Although he reached such a height of power, Oswald was always wonderfully humble, kindly, and generous to the poor and strangers.[122]

And wherever Oswald went, Aidan had an open invitation to go there too—or other Irish-trained leaders like him. Beyond that, there was a rare friendship that grew up between Aidan and Oswald that would be an extraordinary gift in any age and profoundly effective for the advance of the kingdom of God. Ray Simpson described it this way:

> (Aidan and Oswald) weaved in and out of each others' lives as brothers in Christ. A bond formed between them. They became soul friends. And they shared a satisfaction that the flame of Christ was spreading far and wide. Never had Aidan imagined that he could be part of something so amazing, so divine as this mission to bring Christ's ways to so many of the English kingdoms. Were there ever two leaders, before or since, one of the church and the other an earthly ruler, who worked so closely and with such effect to bring God's kingdom on earth as it is in heaven? With

one exception (Penda, the pagan ruler of the large midland kingdom of Mercia—the only major English kingdom to remain outside Oswald's grand alliance) the English lands looked set to become lands of Christ.[123]

But this did not happen by human design. It was an unanticipated gift of God. When Oswald had accepted the Gospel as a teen, he was not a king at all but merely a refugee living in Scotland. The monks of Iona did not minister the Gospel to him because he was of royal blood. The Irish did not use Power-and-Might connections as a means of spreading the Gospel. Instead, they built discipleship communities and invited ordinary people to come and learn how to obey the true King.

Unfortunately, Oswald's reign lasted only nine years before he was killed at age thirty-eight by Penda and the pagan Mercians of central England, who continued to create havoc in all directions. With Oswald's death, however, we do not see the people under his rule suddenly returning to paganism.

Because of Oswald, the Irish from Iona had an opportunity to bring the Gospel of the kingdom to virtually all of England that was under Anglo-Saxon rule, as we shall see in the next chapter. As one writer summarized, "J.B. Lightfoot, a Bishop of Durham during the Victorian era, said wisely that 'Augustine was the apostle of Kent, but Aidan was the apostle of England.'"[124]

That statement proves to be quite literally true, even though it has been also quite literally forgotten. And the upshot is this: it was not Power-and-Might Christianity that succeeded in winning the English to Christ, but the original By-My-Spirit patterns first established by Jesus.

25

AFTER OSWALD

The death of Oswald in 642 was a tragedy beyond comparison. Aidan could not believe that his friend was gone. After Oswald, the two kingdoms of Northumbria became separated again. Bernicia was ruled by Oswald's younger brother, Oswy, who has been described as a nominal Christian. The Deirans to the south asked Oswin, a devout Christian and close friend of Aidan, to rule them.

For a time, Penda continued to threaten Bernicia and its capital at Bamburgh castle, Oswy's royal center. Aidan was on a prayer retreat on the remote Isle of Farne just east of Bamburgh when he noticed a large column of smoke rising up from the castle. Penda's invaders had attacked! They had piled wood against the castle gate and were trying to burn it down! Aidan raised his hands and prayed, hour after hour, "See, Lord, what Penda is doing." As he did this, the wind changed direction, and the smoke blew in the faces of Penda's armies. They retreated, never to return. Bamburgh was saved. Ray Simpson comments, "Aidan learned from such experiences that it is sometimes necessary to take authority in the name of Christ and that this authority is a different order from that imposed by human wills."[125]

King Oswy, ensconced in Bamburgh Castle, then managed to convince Princess Eanfled of the kingdom of Kent, a woman of Roman persuasion, to be his queen in order to form an alliance between north and south. (This despite the fact that Oswy already had married one woman and had several children by others.) He asked Utta, abbot of Gates Head, to fetch the woman from Kent for the royal wedding at York in the building that had been abandoned by Paulinus. Utta came to Aidan, concerned about the danger of such a trip.

> *Utta was fearful lest storms capsize their boat laden with royal goods and the princess. He asked Aidan's advice and his prayers of protection. Aidan blessed a phial of oil and gave it to Utta. He prophesied, "You will meet storms and winds. When they hit you, remember to pour this oil on the sea; the winds will drop at once, the sea will become calm, and will bring you home in serenity." That royal escort was, indeed, caught in a life-endangering storm. At first, they panicked, but as soon as Utta remembered, he poured the oil on the troubled waters. All became still. That incident was the origin of a phrase that passed into the English language: "to pour oil on troubled waters."*[126]

Once the queen was safely ensconced in Bernicia with Oswy, and Aidan had presided at the royal wedding, Aiden proceeded to get to know the lady. She and Oswy had a markedly different attitude toward him and the Church than he had enjoyed with Oswald. It seemed that the two of them looked at the Church as a tool to enhance their own power and prestige. Aidan began to feel that the two of them didn't properly relate to King Jesus or understand the need for obedience to His ways.

Oswin: Similar Name but Different Man

Far different was Oswin, the new king of Deira, who soon became the same kind of soul friend for Aidan that Oswald had been. The two of them thought alike. "Oswin had his own ideas for spreading the faith. He proposed that the following autumn, he gather his youngest thanes at York and create a temporary school when brothers from the monasteries would teach the thanes about prayer, scripture, the desert athletes of the Spirit, forgiveness, the work of the *anamchara*, and spiritual warfare."[127]

It almost seemed as though Oswin was provided to become a kind of younger version of Oswald for Bishop Aiden. In fact, there came a time when Oswin decided to give a warhorse to Aiden to honor him, apparently unaware that Oswald had once tried the very same thing. This time, Aiden received the gift with graciousness—and then gave it away to the next beggar he saw. When Oswin learned of this, he flew at Aidan in a rage.

"How dare you give a beggar the priceless gift I chose for you!" he said. "You could have given that beggar anything—but not the priceless horse I gave to honor you!"

Whereupon Aidan replied, "What are you saying, Oswin? Surely this son of a mare is not more precious to you than that son of God?"

Days later, after much reflection, Oswin approached Aidan, asked his forgiveness, and said, "Never again will I attempt to instruct you about what you will give to any of God's children."[128]

As time passed, trouble began to brew between the two Northumbrian kingdoms, Deira and Bernicia. Oswy had his eye on taking over Deira, and rumor had it that he was planning an attack. Aidan was profoundly troubled by the news and actually had a grievous premonition from God that disaster was about to strike Oswin. But Aidan didn't put it past Oswy to plan such a thing. Oswy wanted to be king of everything, like Oswald. But he was reverting to the old pagan ways to do it. Power and might.

By simply recruiting a larger army than Oswin, he convinced Oswin to hand over Deira voluntarily. Oswin abdicated his throne, disbanded his army, and went into retreat in the home of a friend, a safe house. He had no heart for bloodshed. However, an unknown assassin located Oswin and murdered him. Ray Simpson gives us a picture of Aidan's response when he was told the news:

> *Aidan was in his little cell by the church just outside the bounds of the garrison when the news of Oswin's assassination was brought to him. Sharp pains seized him. He staggered towards the church. He stopped outside it, holding on to the buttress for support. If he was going to die, he wished to die with the breath and beauty of God's creation around him: earth his bed, heaven his home. He clutched his heart in pain, unable to speak. Aides rushed to him. They laid him down. Doctors came. Since they could not move him, they built a little shelter around him, and strapped makeshift bedding to the buttress.*
>
> *...Depression sat heavy upon him. The flame that had impelled him throughout his life began to flicker out. A*

gentle lady in the court named Kemi bathed him. She crooned a song: "Into the arms of Jesus, into the arms of Jesus, into the arms of Jesus, angels, and Mary beside..." He rallied a little. "He may survive," she said. "It is too early to say."

Another visitor came. He spoke to Aidan alone, in a whisper. It was Oswy himself who had paid the assassin to take Oswin's life, like Judas who betrayed Christ for thirty pieces of silver. A shock of pain tore through Aidan's body. He ceased to breathe and lay rigid. They fetched a senior brother. "He is dead," he said.[129]

So ended the life of the man who, more than any other, was responsible for advancing the kingdom of God among Anglo-Saxons: Aidan, "the true Apostle of England."

Who Brought England to Christ?

It is Bede, the first historian in England, who gives us most of our information from this period—and what a rich treasure it is. While Bede is thoroughly convinced that the new Roman version of Christianity is a vastly improved model, rightly replacing the locally owned and operated Celtic thing that British people had been stuck with before then, the more one reads Bede's *Ecclesiastical History*, one cannot but feel that it is the Irish who have won Bede's heart. Even the cover of my copy of this book displays a very Irish-looking manuscript illustration—one of Bede's own works. Looking at this, you would have thought that he himself was Irish.

Roman head. Irish heart.[130]

In fact, Bede himself shows us that it was mostly the Irish who won the Anglo-Saxon kingdoms to Christ. Some of these

Irish came directly from Ireland. For example, Bede shows us Fursey, a visionary who, after two near-death experiences in Ireland (in which he was transported to heaven and returned), he then left Ireland to evangelize the people of East Anglia.[131] He was one of those who simply boarded a coracle and asked God to take him wherever He willed. After weeks at sea, Fursey ended up in East Anglia. This was just the sort of gutsy step of faith that the Irish were known for, ever since the time of Patrick.

What of the West Saxons—Wessex, the kingdom that stretched out west of London as far as Cornwall? When Oswald formed a marital alliance with the West Saxons, an Irish-trained bishop named Agilbert was invited to spread the Gospel there.[132] It was the Irish who won the hearts of the people of Wessex.

Most of the evangelists, however, were men and women discipled by Aidan and others from Iona in the north. These Irish Christians are larger than life, full of encounters with God, battles with demons, miracles, prophecies—and above all, prayer—forceful, faithful, future-shaping prayer. King Jesus was entrusting them with His authority, and they taught Anglo-Saxons how to draw upon that authority to teach the next generation how to be citizens in a new kingdom. Such were Cedd, Chad, Cynibil, and Caelin, four brothers who were among Aidan's first students on Lindisfarne. These became the core of the first generation of Anglo-Saxon leaders to spread the power and love of the kingdom of God among the kingdoms of Old England.

Mercians: the Acid Test!

What about those cruel and warlike Mercians and their king, Penda, who was responsible for so much grief in all directions? How did they become Christians? The answer is: by the evangelism of Irish-trained bishops. The first on the list was Cedd. So powerful was Cedd's influence that King Penda stated publicly his support. As Bede writes: "King Penda himself did not forbid the preaching of the Faith to any even of his own Mercians who wished to listen; but he hated and despised any whom he knew to be insincere in their practice of Christianity once they had accepted it, and said that any who despised the commandments of the God in whom they professed to believe were themselves despicable wretches. This Christian mission was begun two years before Penda's death."[133] Bede never quite says that Penda became a Christian. But Penda did learn to respect Irish Christians.

After Cedd, more of the Irish came to bring Mercia to Christ. Their names were Diuma, Coellach, and Trumhere, forgotten heroes of the kingdom of God. You see how it was actually the Irish who, again and again, brought the transformation of England, kingdom by kingdom, until all were united in Christ.

Finally, to round out the picture, among the East Saxons, Cedd was joined by his brothers, Cynibil, Chad, and Caelin, to once again establish kingdom transformation.

And yet, as effective as they were throughout all the Anglo-Saxon kingdoms (except Kent, under the Roman influence)—they are, all of them, about to be replaced. From my point of view, it is a sad story, yet one that is full of necessary lessons.

26

SPIRITUAL MOTHERS: HILDA

In order to comprehend the tragedy that is about to unfold, let me introduce one of the greatest ladies in the history of Britain. Her name is Hilda. Or just Hild.

From the early days of Brigid, the Irish Church had understood the implications of Joel 2, as quoted by the apostle Peter on the Day of Pentecost—a democratization of the Spirit:

> *Your sons and daughters will prophesy.*
> *...Even on my servants, both men and women*
> *I will pour out my Spirit in those days.*
>
> *Acts 2:17–18*

As to the role of men and women, this expression from the heart of God had blasted the cultural Jewish, not to mention the Roman ideas about "a woman's place." From the beginning, the Irish Church was free to work out for themselves the new democratization of the Spirit among men and women. God had raised up Brigid with such an anointing for Spirit-led leadership that, for generations, women were acknowledged as the equals of men, wherever the Holy Spirit was leading the way, although, of course, their leadership would take different forms and utilize different gifts from that of men. But: "In Christ, there is neither male nor female."

True, only men were given the official role of bishop. But because the Irish Church was not hierarchical, the role of bishop was not necessarily accorded the same high honor as were the roles of abbot and abbess. It was the latter who were in charge of the health and maturing of Christian prayer communities. It was in these communities—from full-fledged monasteries to more informal villages of God—that Christians were challenged to grow up to maturity in Christ, actually following the patterns of life taught by Jesus. It was in these communities that leadership was tested and proven.

So when a woman became an effective abbess, her skill in leadership was widely honored both by women and men. Sometimes, women were in charge of parallel communities— one for men, the other for women. Brigid had started this pattern back in the fifth century. There was no rule, written or unwritten, that said, "You can't have women in charge of men." The apostle Paul's instruction prevailed in these situations: "Be subject one to another out of reverence for Christ" (Ephesians 5:21).[134] Mutual submission.

As the Irish worked out the implications of Joel 2 and Acts 2, the Church came to place a high value on *spiritual mothers*. These were women who gained a reputation for wisdom in the things of God. The honor accorded to spiritual mothers was a unique feature of the Irish church, as the Holy Spirit moved to develop Spirit-anointed leadership among both men and women.

Among the English?

When Aidan brought Irish Christianity to the Anglo-Saxons, he found a culture that offered very little to most women by way of leadership. One of his challenges was to create a place for spiritual mothers in England.

God was revolutionizing the relations between men and women, promoting mutual honor. The concept of mutual honor began to penetrate Anglo-Saxon culture in the time of Aidan. This, along with the freeing of slaves, was revolutionizing Power-and-Might cultures with the love of God, softening the hard edges of all human relationships as they emerged from the cruelties of the god of this world. Power and might.

In England, the beginnings of this revolution happened during Oswald's reign, when a woman named Bega sought sanctuary in his realms. She was fleeing her father, a pagan king in Ireland, who wanted her to marry a prince from another tribe. She refused, wanting to devote herself to Christ alone, and the prince raped her in his anger. Deeply wounded, she fled and received sanctuary in Rheged, a kingdom now aligned with Oswald's Northumbria, to the west.

During her journey there, she happened upon an Irish hermitage that consisted of three women. They took her in and gave her shelter for a short time. In her conversation with them, they explained that they were bound together by their common relationship with Christ, symbolized by a bracelet, which they presented to her. They explained that the bracelet was really a ring, a ring large enough for the three of them to get their fingers through together. "We call ourselves 'the fellowship of the ring,'" they explained.[135] They were so moved by Bega's story that they gave her the bracelet, which bound her to them by the fellowship of the ring.

She moved on, crossed over to Rheged, and built a house of prayer there. Bega became one of the early "spiritual mothers" in Anglo-Saxon country.[136] The fellowship of the ring was to challenge the power and might culture that had created such division between men and women from time immemorial. For the rest of Bega's life, the ring symbolized her connection with, and indebtedness to, the move of God among Irish women, which she was now bringing to the Anglo-Saxons.[137]

Hilda

There were several other forerunners for women's leadership among the Anglo-Saxons, but the most famous of all spiritual mothers (in any age) was Hilda, the niece of King Edwin. This young lady was one of many thousands of Northumbrians baptized, early on, by the Roman bishop, Paulinus. When Edwin was killed, and Paulinus fled south to a safer sanctuary, Hilda was one of the few who did not instantly revert to paganism. For some reason, the new faith meant more to her than to the others, and she continued to embrace it.

It was Aidan and his Irish friends who then discipled her and showed her the true lifestyle of the kingdom of God so that she adopted the culture of Irish Christians, even though she had been baptized by Romans. So when Oswy eventually became king and brought Enfleda up from Kent to be his wife, Hilda did not adopt the Roman customs that her relative, Enfleda, brought with her to Northumbria. And when Hilda eventually decided to become a prayer leader, Aidan made the decision to invest in her, to train her for leadership in a house of prayer for women in Northumbria. Ray Simpson observes:

> *Not for him the icy separation between men and women that marked the Roman churches and even the desert fathers. Hilda was the woman who could make his vision (for spiritual mothers in England) a reality, and nothing must get in the way.*

> *We do not know what messages were relayed and what discussions took place, but we know that Hilda came (to Aidan for training). It indicates a degree of belief in Aidan and what he stood for, so strong that she was willing to set aside protocol, family, and security and risk all for the greatest adventure of her life. Paulinus, who died about that time, would have turned in his grave.*[138]

The long and the short of it was this: Hilda, rising up from the discipling of Aidan and his Irish friends, became the greatest Christian leader of her generation in Anglo-Saxon country, respected not only by Irish leaders but even by Romans (if only because she was of royal blood). Under the mentoring of Aidan and his successors at Lindisfarne, there rose up a house of prayer at Whitby for men and women, men living on one side, women on the other, and the prayer chapel in the center. Its fame would equal that of Iona and of Lindisfarne— and Hilda every bit as respected a leader as Columba or Aidan.

Perhaps the best way to convey the wisdom and power of this woman is to tell a story related by Bede.[139]

Caedmon

There was a gardener named Caedmon who worked in the Whitby abbey, a man who not only tended the gardens but cleaned up after the animals. He was not a Christian but worked at what today would be called minimum wage, doing the least honorable kind of work available to people of no skill. He would hear the praises of God sung by the men and women of the abbey, and he would say to himself, "I wish I could sing like that."

One night, Caedmon had a dream in which a man appeared to him and said, "Caedmon, sing me a song."

Caedmon replied, "Sir, I don't know how to sing."

The man replied, "Nevertheless, you shall sing to me."

Caedmon, wondering, asked, "What should I sing about?"

"Sing about the Creation of all things," came the reply.

Caedmon opened his mouth, and out came the following song:

"Praise we the Fashioner now of Heaven's fabric,
The majesty of his might and his mind's wisdom,
Work of the world-warden, worker of all wonders,
How he the Lord of Glory everlasting,
Wrought first for the race of men Heaven as a rooftree,
Then made the Middle Earth to be their mansion."[140]

The following day, Caedmon told his overseer about what had happened, how he had suddenly received an ability to write and sing praise to God. The overseer brought him directly to Hilda, who, in turn, brought him to her team of leaders. All heard his story and agreed that Jesus had revealed Himself to Caedmon and given him an extraordinary gifting of the Spirit. They assigned certain brothers to teach him the way of Jesus, all the while giving him an opportunity to practice the gifting of the Holy Spirit that Jesus had bestowed.

The result was that Caedmon became the first known Christian hymn-writer in England, and the above hymn, the first known Christian hymn in English. More than that, Caedmon was, overnight, lifted from the lowest echelon of Anglo-Saxon society to one of the highest—for bards were honored above almost everyone. The King had a high destiny for Caedmon, and Hilda knew how to make that destiny come true.

This was the power that Jesus was unleashing into the Anglo-Saxon culture—the power to give people kingdom destinies by the anointing of the Holy Spirit. And Hilda knew how to align herself with the King and to recognize spiritual gifts as they emerged among her people. She saw what the King wanted, and she understood how to keep from getting in His way. In the new world she was building, you could become almost anything once it was established that God was in it. Hilda had embraced this destiny for herself—with Aidan's help. Then she turned and helped everyone else to do the same. It was this liberty that was winning the hearts of whole nations to honor and worship the King.

But then…something happened to that vision.

27

WILFRID AND THE SYNOD OF WHITBY

During Aidan's last three years, there came a student to his school named Wilfrid. This young man became aware that there were other possibilities that the Christian world offered him than that offered by the Irish locals. Queen Enfleda told him about the splendor of the Roman Church. Fascinated, Wilfrid asked permission of his teachers to go to Rome and learn from the Romans. Ray Simpson describes the result:

> *Permission was readily given to such requests at the Lindis-farne monastery. Boys at the school were not required to become monks, they could feel free to do whatever they felt called to. Wilfrid was to fall in love with Rome and all things Roman: its large buildings, its artifacts, libraries, and canonical regulations, the splendor and power of bishops and clergy. For the rest of his life he expended his powers to make the church in England like that.*[141]

When Wilfrid returned from Rome in 658, one thing he had clearly learned was how to use his connections with royalty to elbow his way into church positions. He convinced Enfleda's son Alchfrith to expel the Irish from the monastery at Ripon and appoint him as abbot in their place.

(This way of using royalty to wedge one's way into church positions will prove to have its limitations. Twice during the course of Wilfrid's career, he is going to run into trouble with the next king of Northumbria, Egfrid, who is going to drive him out of his position. Twice, Wilfrid will have to make trips to Rome to plead his case, and then Egfrid is going to discover that he will have to take Wilfrid back.[142] England is having to learn how to be connected to the wider Church, full of people of a very different spirit from Aidan.)

The Quartodeciman Controversy

Wilfrid's career is going to take a turn for the better in 664 when the aging King Oswy begins to express dismay at the conflict between the Irish and Roman traditions concerning the dating of Easter. He has learned to celebrate Easter in the Irish way, which still used the Jewish dating of Passover (on the 14th of Nisan, regardless of the day of the week).

Oswy's wife Enfleda, however, had learned the Roman way. The Romans had changed the tradition to fit the pattern of regular Sunday observance—so that Easter always fell on Sundays. (And so: all of us today.)

Oswy wanted the matter resolved, so he asked for a synod to decide the matter. Let the Irish argue their side; let the Romans argue theirs. Then Oswy would make a decision for his family—and for his entire realm, which now included (through alliances) much of England. Some say that, through Enfleda's influence, Oswy had already made up his mind, but he needed to make a show of objectivity because he needed to keep peace with Dalriata and the Iona people, who did things the Irish way.

Let's push Pause again to add a little historical perspective. The question of the dating of Easter had been roiling for centuries. Known as the Quartodeciman controversy, the issue had boiled up at the end of the second century when Pope Victor decided to excommunicate everyone who didn't go along with the Roman practice. This included almost all the churches of Asia Minor, Cilicia, Syria, Judea, and Mesopotamia, who felt that what was good enough for Jesus was good enough for them. As my friend, Dr. David Rudolph, Director of Messianic Jewish Studies at The King's University, has pointed out, "Far from being a minor schismatic group, Gentile Christians who celebrated Passover on Nissan 14 stretched across a vast geographic region that represented the heartland of apostolic Christianity."[143] Pope Victor was taking it upon himself to change the practice of Jesus and the apostles of the Church to fit Roman thinking. And he was prepared to excommunicate all those who disagreed with him.[144]

Irenaeus was appalled at Victor's actions and wrote a letter to Victor. Bear in mind that Irenaeus' mentor in the faith was Polycarp, who celebrated Passover according to the Jewish tradition, on Nissan 14, and Irenaeus was likely the main person who conveyed this tradition to the Celts. Ray Simpson summarizes: "Irenaeus' letter advocate(d) that Easter should be on a Sunday but plead(ed) that diversity of practice be respected."[145] This was always the position of the Celtic Church on most issues—that there must be room for diversity and mutual respect among Christians. Humility demands this.

What we see already growing up in the Roman Church is the practice of ex-communication to force uniformity. This way of dealing with issues was utterly foreign to Celtic

Christians until the Romans introduced it in seventh-century England. The Roman Church had re-interpreted the "keys of the kingdom" passage of Matthew 16:19 from its original meaning. When Jesus said, "I will give you the keys of the kingdom of heaven; whatever you bind on earth will be bound in heaven,"[146] the Romans no longer made reference to the Gates of Hell grotto in Paneas. They are imagining Jesus giving Peter (and therefore, themselves) the right to close off heaven from *people*, as they so choose. What started out as an authority to set people free from demonic power is now becoming the right of the Roman Church to threaten people with hell by excommunicating them from the One True Church—and so exclude them from heaven. This idea is going to drop like a bolt from the blue into the English Church, which, somehow or other, has never heard it before.

Or so it seems, as the Synod of Whitby played out.

The Synod of Whitby

Mother Hilda was invited to host the Synod at Whitby, perhaps because she had roots in both the Roman and Celtic traditions but also because she was so highly respected as a leader. And, she was of royal blood. Bishop Colman of Lindisfarne was invited to argue the Irish side of the Easter issue. There were two men who, though trained by the Irish, were now throwing their sympathies with Rome. The most prestigious of these, Agilbert, Bishop of Wessex, was invited to argue for Rome. But, because of his difficulty with the language, he deferred to the other: Wilfrid.

Ray Simpson comments:

Accommodating these guests must have challenged the monastery to its limits. Not long after his appearance at Whitby, Wilfrid would refuse to be consecrated a bishop on Northumbrian soil because he thought that those in the Irish tradition were too cavalier in their observance of the minutiae of canon law. Instead he would be consecrated on the continent by three bishops in full regalia, and he would instruct nine priests to carry him aloft on a throne![147]

Wilfrid showed up in all his splendor to present the glory of Rome, as over against poor Colman, who, though he was a bishop, was dressed as a simple Irish monk. They were ready to argue their case before the King, in a room that held 300 people (large, by the standards of Northumbria).

Bede tells us what happened at the Synod. Cedd was appointed to translate between the Irish and English. Cedd was the eldest of those four brothers who had been among Aidan's first students. Now he was a master at interpreting both sides of the two cultures to each other. (The idea that the Irish were stuck in their own little provincial world was the opposite of the truth. It was the Irish who had taken the trouble to learn Anglo-Saxon language and culture in order to present the Gospel of the kingdom to them. But those on the Roman side still struggled with the language barrier. The irony of this situation will become clear as we go along.)

With all gathered together, and the King appropriately seated on a kind of throne in the middle of the crowd, Corman was given the nod to start the debate for the Irish. He explained that the Irish observed Easter the way they did because that is how the apostle John had done, and they were doing as he did, as taught by Jesus Himself.

Wilfrid replied to this seemingly incontrovertible point as follows:

> *Our Easter customs are those that we have seen universally observed in Rome, where the blessed Apostles Peter and Paul lived, taught, suffered, and are buried. We have also seen the same customs generally observed throughout Italy and Gaul when we travelled through these countries for study and prayer. Furthermore, we have learnt that Easter is observed by men of different nations and languages at one and the same time, in Africa, Asia, Egypt, Greece, and throughout the world wherever the Church has spread. The only people who stupidly contend against the whole world are those Irishmen and their partners in obstinacy, the Picts and Britons, who inhabit only a portion of these the two uttermost islands of the ocean.*[148]

Colman replied that John was not a stupid man. Eventually, after much argument between the two sides lasting days, he went on to hold up the great Columba, who was surely to be revered for his sanctity, his miracles, and the power of his life.

To this, Wilfrid replied:

> *…With regard to your Father Columba and his followers, whose holiness you claim to imitate and whose rules and customs you claim to have been supported by heavenly signs, I can only say that when many shall say to our Lord at the day of Judgement: "Have we not prophesied in thy name, and cast out devils, and done many wonderful works?" the Lord will reply, "I never knew you." Far be it from me to*

apply these words to your fathers; for it is more just to believe good rather than evil of those whom one does not know. So I do not deny that they are true servants of God and dear to Him, and that they loved Him in primitive simplicity but in devout sincerity. Nor do I think that their ways of keeping Easter were seriously harmful, so long as no one came to show them a more perfect way to follow. Indeed, I feel certain that, if any Catholic reckoner had come to them, they would readily have accepted his guidance, as we know that they readily observed such of God's ordinances as they already knew. But you and your colleagues are most certainly guilty of sin if you reject the decrees of the Apostolic See, indeed of the universal Church, which are confirmed by Holy Writ. For, although your Fathers were holy men, do you imagine that they, a few men in a corner of a remote island, are to be preferred before the universal Church of Christ throughout the world? And even if your Columba— or, may I say, ours also if he was the servant of Christ—was a Saint potent in miracles, can he take precedence before the most blessed Prince of the Apostles, to whom our Lord said: "Thou art Peter, and upon this rock I will build my Church, and the gates of hell shall not prevail against it, and I will give unto thee the keys of the kingdom of heaven.[149]

…to which the King asked Colman if the Lord had spoken those same words to Columba. The answer: No.

To which the King replied, "Since Peter is the one who opens the gates of heaven, I shall not contradict him." And without delay, Oswy declared for Rome. And against the Irish.

Implications Unimagined

That decision to choose Rome and reject Ireland—based on the alleged power to open and close heaven to people—was to have implications that would last for centuries. Rome now gained the right to dictate every manner of detail into the lives of all Christians. For example, the Roman monks (Benedictines) had decided to cut their hair in a tonsure (with its bald spot at the top and a fringe of hair all around). The Irish way was now declared to be "wrong." All monks from now on would wear a Roman tonsure.

Likewise, Rome had gained the right to declare Peter the "prince" of apostles, higher and more important, for example, than John. Who cares about John, anyway? It's Peter who will get you into heaven. And Peter is buried in Rome. Why is this important? Because Peter passes along his apostolic authority to Roman popes. So now, in Britain, it will be Rome, with its power to excommunicate, who will gain a presence and authority on behalf of all Christians everywhere. And the Romans moved in to press their advantage.

The implications of this transition in the seventh century will be absolutely enormous. Eventually, it will transition all of the British Isles from the original pattern, the "By-My-Spirit" pattern, to a "Power-and-Might" pattern that will become normal, then universal, as the vast majority of people in the British Isles and elsewhere assume that what Rome teaches and lives out is surely what Jesus intended all along.

Within the year, vast numbers of Irish, the Christians who had actually brought transformation to pagan Britain, will have left to return to Ireland or to Iona. A few will remain and try to work within the new system, which has become quietly hostile to them and dishonoring of their greatest leaders.

Bruce Ritchie summarizes:

At Whitby, Wilfrid had been the main protagonist for the Roman Church over against the Columban tradition, and he insinuated doubt about the validity of Columba's ministry. Wilfrid was a brilliant if an unscrupulous debater. He lambasted what he saw as the arrogance of the Irish Church in thinking it was correct and the rest of the Christian world was wrong....Wilfrid knew that if he could undermine Columba's personal spiritual legitimacy, then his opponents would be seriously weakened. He therefore hinted heavily that Columba was well-meaning but misguided. Crucially, Columba was suspect in that he had only been an abbot and never a bishop. In the Roman Church, bishops were leaders, strategists, authority figures, and the men whose advice and direction could be followed with confidence. Abbots were not mentioned in Scripture, but bishops were. Abbots were not part of an apostolic succession in an unbroken line from the first apostles, but bishops were. ...Columba had never been ordained to the office of bishop.[150]

The Power of Dishonor

Hilda was crushed by this outcome. The people who had discipled her, the ones who had actually given her Jesus, who had believed in her, trained her, and opened the door for her to be a leader—these were now vilified, ridiculed, dishonored, and rejected. She sensed the depth of the disaster that had just happened, yet there was nothing she could do about it. Her calling was to practice love and to pray. Yet, for some reason, God had allowed what she felt was a great tragedy, and with each passing year, the depth of the tragedy would become clearer.

For the rest of her life, there came a fever that afflicted her, an actual sickness that never left her. Was she somehow reflecting in her body a sickness that had entered her beloved England? The Holy Spirit, though a fountain of healing virtue, did not always heal every sickness, as Jesus had done while on earth, and would do again when He comes to restore all things. The Holy Spirit was given as an "earnest" (Ephesians 1:14) of all that God would eventually do at the restoration of all things.[151] But for now, we live in an imperfect world, where we "see through a glass darkly." And just as there was no relief from the fever for the rest of her life, neither was there relief from the grief over her beloved Irish. But God is a rewarder of those who diligently seek Him.

The Iona community, which for decades had been sending out Irish monks to evangelize the Anglo-Saxons, now began to receive them back in droves. There is no doubt that Adamnan, the abbot of Iona, wrote his *Life of Columba* because he sensed that the great hero of the Irish Church was being unfairly demeaned. Just like Patrick, centuries before. Adamnan wanted to defend him and portray him before the new narrative, about the heroism of the Roman Church winning the British Isles to Christ, swept their hero completely out of remembrance.

And with him, all the other Irish heroes of the faith, as well.

28

THE BY-MY-SPIRIT KING

To my mind, this is a poor place to end a story. If it were a play, it would be a tragedy. Not because the Romans won, but because a Power-and-Might lifestyle replaced the original By-My-Spirit lifestyle. That is the tragedy behind the Synod of Whitby.

From my point of view, Satan opposed the Christians by beguiling them to put their trust in the wrong power source. Worldly power had already been spoiled by the evil one. God poured out His Spirit on the Church to provide a safe *alternative power source*. But what God calls safe and what we call safe are two different things.

Just to Summarize

For seven centuries, the first Christians developed a healthy caution toward the deceptiveness of human thinking and self-will. We have seen how King Jesus had continued to pour out the Holy Spirit with powerful anointings and awakenings, generation after generation, first in the Egyptian desert, then in Celt country. The seven ingredients of the By-My-Spirit lifestyle spread west as the kingdom of God overtook demonized territories and set people free from the lust and blood-lust inherent in pagan cultures. Leaders like Pachomius,

Evagrius, Patrick, and Columba became skilled at confronting demonic power and gaining victory over dark forces of the spirit world. Spirit-filled people flooded into pagan tribes to bring love and to set people free from slavery of all sorts, including the institution of slavery itself.

This, at the beginning, was very good news. People were hungry for this. Whole cultures wanted it and recognized its goodness when it appeared in their towns and cities. This was how Christian cultures were birthed in the first place. Nobody in our story of kingdom advance forced Christianity on anyone. Africans, Celts, and Anglo-Saxons received the new faith willingly because they saw that it was an improvement for them. Their lives were being wonderfully transformed by the seven-part lifestyle taught by Jesus.

The seven-part lifestyle was based on the assumption that the Holy Spirit, not worldly power, would be the power source for the kingdom of God. To review, the kingdom of God requires us to co-operate with God's thoughts in the following seven ways:

1. Surrender our lives to the King
2. Ask for the Holy Spirit
3. Let God write His laws on our hearts
4. Practice Christlike humility and servanthood
5. Pursue love and unity
6. Pray much—this is the authority of the kingdom.
7. Utilize daily the direct connection with God that Jesus purchased for us on the cross.

As the Roman Church began to lose their grip on these lifestyle ingredients, the Desert Fathers and Mothers tightened theirs. For seven centuries, the Western Church earnestly walked out the By-My-Spirit pattern, as the Gospel of the kingdom spread all the way to Ireland. The Celts discovered that the life of surrender to the Spirit of God is rich with miracles and adventure. For centuries, their greatest heroes lived this adventure and taught others to do the same. The goal was not necessarily to have more miracles in their lives but to be restored to God, to know His love, and to let that love course through them to affect all relationships.

But in order to maintain this love, they had to fight an enemy who is dead-set to destroy it. This enemy works through deception. He may call his ways "love," yet the end result is always hurt and bitterness. And so the Desert Fathers and Mothers, and then the Celts learned to be on their guard, to pinpoint the deadly thoughts that would invariably dead-end the pursuit of love. They did this through houses of prayer, discipleship communities, and soul friendships. These were the methods by which the kingdom of God transformed societies.

Then Rome turned it all into a religion fit for kings. This transformation-in-reverse did not happen overnight. It came by fits and starts, and it would take several centuries before the new imperial religion would become a new normal. But for 700 years, the By-My-Spirit pattern prevailed as the normal pattern for Christians. Only at the end of that period did Power-and-Might Christianity replace the original pattern and become normal for another 700 years.

To my way of thinking, the Synod of Whitby in 664 AD was the turning point, at least for the British Isles. It was then that the Church in Britain made a formal declaration for Rome. Then Bede, in his *Ecclesiastical History*, sealed the deal in 731. While Bede appreciated individual leaders and the spirit of the Irish Church, it was necessary by the eighth century to honor the Roman Church as the One True Church—with its basilicas, its religious hierarchy, and the seemingly universal acceptance of its power to excommunicate.

Only by hindsight can we see an underlying tragedy here, a tragedy that would have devastating consequences. It would take another 700 years before large numbers of Christians would recognize that something, somewhere, had gone terribly wrong with the vision of the Christian Church. And their efforts to reform the Church, and to return to the By-My-Spirit lifestyle, would cost many of them their lives.

As a Reformed Christian, I was raised to believe that the Great Reformation was the beginning of a return to a biblical vision of life and of God's purposes in history. But, once again, if that is so, the transition back to the original vision of the By-My-Spirit King has been painfully slow, taking centuries. It is as though we don't quite understand the nature of this virus that attacks the lungs of the Body of Christ. Our diagnostics have let us down again and again.

The good news is: the transition has been happening, even though it has been painfully slow. God has poured out His Spirit in waves of spiritual awakening, and these have included, at times, the Roman Church. These seasons of God's power (which I will describe in Volume Two) have fulfilled the prophecy the apostle Peter gave us at the beginning: "times of refreshing from the presence of the Lord" that flow from massive repentance.

The Third Great Awakening

I believe that we are standing at the front end of a great awakening just now. Many today are speaking of it. Tim Sheets, for example, recently prophesied that this next "Third Great Awakening" will combine the streams of all previous great awakenings. Many Christians throughout the world today are saying this, and believing for just such a fulfillment of this promise. Some of those who speak like this are aware of the Azusa Revival, others, of Count Von Zinzendorf and the Moravians, others, of the evangelical awakenings that go back to the Scottish Reformation.

But the transformational power of God goes back in history farther than any of those moves of the Holy Spirit. I felt it was important to tell the story of kingdom advance as the documents reveal it in the first seven centuries of the Christian era, so we could grasp the whole story of kingdom advance and the spiritual awakening of nations from the start. I felt it would be profitable to ask the simple question: What did God do? How did the kingdom of God actually advance west throughout Europe and into the British Isles? Surely we could learn some lessons from those times to help us respond to the moves of God throughout the earth today?

If this is true, then there is one lesson I believe we can lay hold of: God has declared for the By-My-Spirit lifestyle, and not the other. There is not an ounce of Power-and-Mightism in the plans of God. If there is anything that our history with God teaches, it is this simple lesson.

We, the people God has created to love Him, like to create systems that we can control. But the kingdom of God begins with an act of surrender—and the *loss of control*. Can we believe that if we get in our own personal coracle without a paddle, we will end up just exactly where God wants us? Right at that point of decision, every one of us stands on the verge of helping or hindering the advance of the kingdom of God.

29

My Own Story of Kingdom *Dunamis*

Let me tell a personal story of entering into this kingdom adventure, if you please, to illustrate the relevance. I also want to correct a false impression that many are likely to take away from these stories I have told.

Back in the 1970s, God was pouring out His Spirit in the Charismatic movement. During this season of spiritual awakening, the mainline, historic denominations were included in a re-introduction of the promise of the baptism of the Holy Spirit. Presbyterians, Methodists, Baptists, Episcopalians, and Roman Catholics were getting baptized in the Holy Spirit, often with an experience of speaking in tongues to go along with it.[152] My wife Carla and I were part of that.

In 1972, on the Day of Pentecost, Carla and I surrendered our lives ("Let go and let God") and asked for the Holy Spirit by faith in the promises of God. God responded in amazing ways almost immediately.

After our own encounter with the Holy Spirit in Oregon, Carla and I made a trip back to the Midwest and shared our experience with both sets of parents. In Madison, Wisconsin, where I grew up, I told my parents about my encounter with God. My Dad's only comment was: "So, you've become a holy roller now?" Not so encouraging!

We then went to a town near Ann Arbor, Michigan, to tell my wife's family about our encounter with God. My father-in-law pastored a Presbyterian church there.

Ann Arbor, just then, was enjoying an amazing outbreak of the Holy Spirit among Catholics. We attended one of the weekly gatherings of the Word of God Community in a local gymnasium in Ann Arbor and were amazed at the power and goodness of the Holy Spirit that was manifesting among Catholics. Though some old-line Pentecostals said that Catholics couldn't possibly receive the baptism of the Holy Spirit, it was clear to us that they could. We were quite impressed and signed up for a subscription to *New Covenant* magazine to stay abreast of what God was doing among Catholics. I also read Catholic charismatic writers like Kilian McDonnell and Francis McNutt, as well as hands-on leaders like Ralph Martin. Eventually, I designed a Life-in-the-Spirit seminar patterned after the Catholic Life-in-the-Spirit seminar written up by Steve Clark. Ralph Martin and Steve Clark were leaders of the Word of God Community.

After returning home, I learned that my Dad had started attending a Catholic charismatic prayer group at Our Lady Queen of Peace Catholic Church in Madison. My parents had been founding leaders in a nearby Presbyterian church for decades. Yet my father was so spiritually hungry that he was willing to go to a Catholic charismatic prayer group to seek this new thing that God was doing. Who knew? The Catholics included him in their prayer meetings and helped him discover the person and work of the Holy Spirit. Similarly, my wife and I sometimes attended a Catholic charismatic group that had sprung up in Corvallis, Oregon.

My mom, however, was not at all happy about this turn of events. Her world was spinning out of control, and she wanted my dad to just return to his normal Presbyterian routine.

One day, in December 1972, Mom was stricken with a brain hemorrhage. She was hospitalized at St. Mary's Hospital in Madison, where the diagnosis was confirmed by a spinal tap. They found blood in her spinal fluid. She had nonstop headaches; she was in bad shape.

Dad told his Catholic prayer group about the crisis, and the leaders of the group decided to go up to her hospital room and pray for Mom with the laying on of hands. Mom could not say no. The result of this visit was that my mother was instantly healed of the brain hemorrhage, a back disability she had suffered for years, and an ulcer. All healed in a moment! The following day, she walked out of St. Mary's Hospital totally well. The power of the King had walked right into her life, and she became a new woman.

In those days, Charismatics were having huge annual gatherings to celebrate God. These mass meetings included Protestants, Pentecostals, Word-of-Faith people, and, yes, Catholics, all worshiping together, tens of thousands in one gigantic convention center, all together in the Lord. It was a sight to behold. I will never forget it. How I would love to see that sight again!

Misguided judgmentalism
As I have taught *Glory Through Time* around the world, some people have wondered if I am anti-Roman Catholic. If the story I tell were to end here, where this book ends, I suppose you could get that impression. My desire in telling this story is to show the pathology of God's Church at the start, and

the virus of Power-and-Might faith that has afflicted us all these years. You have only to follow the story a little farther into history to see how universal this affliction is. It is not a Catholic virus; it is a human virus that potentially afflicts all Christians.

In fact, those who have written most eloquently about the deceptiveness of Power-and-Might culture have been Catholics. I have quoted Lord Acton—a Catholic.[153] I have also referred frequently to Malachi Martin and his book, *The Decline and Fall of the Roman Church*. Martin had no sympathy for the Great Reformation; he was a faithful Roman Catholic. But he articulated in detail the poison of what I am calling Power-and-Might Christianity and grieved over the harm that it has done over the centuries within his own denomination.

J.R.R. Tolkien was a Roman Catholic and the most eloquent writer of all. *The Lord of the Rings* has a great deal to say about the pursuit of worldly power and might. When we slip the Ring of Power onto our own finger, two things happen. We disappear. Then the evil one notices us and comes after us. We can become fascinated with the Ring of Power and, if we do, we end up like Gollum. Any of us, potentially, can become Gollum. The Church was meant to be a Fellowship of the Ring, raised up to destroy the Ring of Power. And yet, the temptation of the Ring is always tempting, enticing, attracting.

In the end, the truth emerges: the best thing we can do with the Ring of Power is to get rid of it. Toss it into the lake of fire. Just destroying the Ring of Power, in itself, is a heroic deed, which, if we can achieve it, becomes the greatest mercy of all. *The Lord of the Rings* is more than idle fantasy. Like all good fiction, it tells the truth to those who are willing to listen.

The closer we come to the pursuit of God, the less likely are we to cast judgment on any church or denomination. I appreciate, for example, the writings of Frank Bartleman in the searching that led to the Azusa Street Revival. Early in Bartleman's quest for a fuller revelation of Jesus, he reflects on the state of twentieth-century churches:

> *How far we have fallen from the early pattern, and even from the type of the church, Israel. We are so far from it that we scarcely recognize the real thing. Even the Catholic Church, though formal, is ahead of us in this. The difficulty and shame is that we are hopelessly divided.*[154]

This beginning insight helped contribute to the spiritual search that led to the Azusa Street Revival. Oh, that we could get this passion back again.

30

Takeaways

As I have mentioned, many prophecies today speak of an end-time great awakening, often referred to as "The Third Great Awakening." I will include some of these prophecies in Volume Two of this work. There is a long history of these prophecies going back decades, even centuries, but they have multiplied and grown more specific in the last several years.

I agree with these prophecies. I believe we are about to discover, once again, that there is a King of the Nations, the By-My-Spirit King, who is in control of history. His name is Yeshua, a.k.a. Jesus. History is moving inexorably to His conclusion, and none of us can stop this progress, even if we wanted to, though we do have the power to reject it for ourselves.

My goal in asking, "What did God do" during the first seven centuries of the Christian era has been to establish a solid core of facts, and a story from those facts, to show that the kingdom of God is a transformational power in which the Presence of God comes to "restore all things." Without some attempt to tell the story of the previous spiritual awakenings throughout history, we would have no idea how to evaluate these current prophecies. Are they merely a weird fantasy spawned in the mind of some demented and self-deceived "prophet?" Or are they the outworking of a pattern that has been surfacing and resurfacing all along throughout our history? I believe the latter is the truth.

Restoration is the ultimate goal, as my Messianic Jewish friends from Tikkun International continue to emphasize during their annual conferences. Tikkun is Hebrew for "restore." Their anchor for this name is Acts 3:19-21, which has also been the anchor for all my research in *Glory Through Time*.

Once we have a clear understanding of how the kingdom of God spread to the West from Jerusalem, I felt we would be in a better position to draw some conclusions about the kingdom of God for today. What lessons, then, can we draw from these stories of ancient times that would apply to the present and to this imminent global "Third Great Awakening" being prophesied today? Jesus is the same, yesterday, today, and forever.

Here are some of the more salient takeaways from my research.

1. It Begins With Surrender to the King

The kingdom of God is the By-My-Spirit kingdom. Its power and authority do not run along normal human pathways of power and control. To enter this kingdom requires an act of surrender. It does not require an act of taking control and using power, required under all other kingdoms and systems of government. Just the opposite. Surrender is the opposite of control. You cannot think your way into this kingdom; you can only surrender your way into it.

Constantinian Christianity failed to grasp this distinction, and it set up a competition among Christians between two ideas of what the kingdom of God is. This competition cuts across all denominations and enters into every church as our most basic controversy.

We are all Constantine, the emperor who, unfortunately, never took time to listen to God, he was so busy being Emperor. It seemed to him that if he could develop the kingdom of God into a religion that would unite his empire into a new Christian entity, everyone would win. The Church would no longer be persecuted. And he would be able to more readily unite his empire. Surely he had the best of intentions in making Christianity the official religion of the Roman Empire. But, as we have seen, that is not what the King of Kings had already decreed.

The Power-and-Might twist was not the improvement Constantine thought it would be, and it did a great deal of damage to the integrity of the Gospel of the kingdom throughout the ensuing centuries. I will show the tragic result in Volume Two of this work, as Power-and-Might Christians, emboldened by the Stuart kings and the doctrine of the Divine Right of Kings, drove wave after wave of spiritually awakened Christians out of Britain and across the Atlantic ocean to America. This established a westward momentum that continues to this day in the Back to Jerusalem movement. It is this westward momentum that I will trace in Volume Two.

The By-My-Spirit lifestyle begins when, for one reason or another, we come to appreciate that God's thoughts are higher than ours, and so we become willing to listen to them. We enter into a lifestyle of paying attention. After all, God sees the complexity of all things, including the spirit realm, and He is actually smarter than we are. God sometimes has to move heaven and earth to get us to the place where we respect His thoughts enough to listen to them.

It is only then that we will consider personally surrendering our will to the power and authority of the Holy Spirit, by whom Jesus, at present, rules this world. Personal surrender is Square One in advancing the kingdom of God in our own lives. It is still perfectly true that the person who saves his life will lose it, but whoever loses their life for Jesus will find it (Matthew 16:25). This is the most basic lesson we can gain from those who advanced the kingdom of God during those early years. Surrender to the adventure.

2. The Church, A House of Prayer

God, from the start, has been looking for a Royal Priesthood (Exodus 19:5-6; 1 Peter 2:5, 9; Revelation 1:6) and a House of Prayer (Isaiah 56:7, Matthew 21:13). Those who develop this calling into a religious system under their control have already misunderstood what God is after. He wants us to stop and draw near to Him. It is just that simple. Those who advanced the kingdom of God at first were those who had discovered this basic principle: "Draw near to God and He will draw near to you" (James 4:8).

Originally, the Church was a house of prayer full of people who wanted to learn this very simple principle. The Bible showed them what God had done to enable this to happen: the death on a cross; the torn curtain; the ascension of Jesus; the Holy Spirit poured out; the evidence God gave for a powerful presence on earth that hadn't been there before. The first Christians weren't trying to develop an impressive Sunday religion fit for kings. They were trying out a lifestyle that raised ordinary people up and brought them near to The King. The kingdom of God was profoundly different from anything that had occurred before, and it is not surprising that Constantine misunderstood it. It is a divine thought. Not a human one.

Even Antony thought, at first, that he could challenge Satan with sheer bravado. Then God taught him how to draw near to God and learn to listen to Him in the desert. It took him twenty years to learn this one lesson. Listening to God is better than bravado. Once he had learned to listen, he also learned to aggressively destroy the power of the god of this world by the gifts of the Spirit, Christian prayer, and spiritual warfare.[155] And once he had learned these lessons, he was able to teach others also.

3. Discipleship Communities

The Church is not primarily a religious institution—if we take our clues from the early years. It is a network of discipleship communities constantly dividing and multiplying. King Jesus Himself decreed this. In these communities, those who are more experienced in walking with the King can help other younger believers to do as they do. The early Church offered people these opportunities:

> *Let us draw near to God with a sincere heart and with the full assurance that faith brings, having our hearts sprinkled to cleanse us from a guilty conscience and having our bodies washed with pure water. Let us hold unswervingly to the hope we profess, for he who promised is faithful. And let us consider how we may spur one another on toward love and good deeds, not giving up meeting together, as some are in the habit of doing, but encouraging one another—and all the more as you see the Day approaching.*
>
> *Hebrews 10:22-25*

The Church, at the start, was charged with establishing the pattern of "faith working through love," a coupling together of two ingredients into the lives of all kingdom citizens (Galatians 5:6). To which the apostle Paul added purity of heart and conscience: "The goal of this command is love, which comes from a pure heart, a good conscience and a sincere faith" (1 Timothy 1:5). Easy to say. Not always easy to do. Most of us need help, especially at the beginning of our walk. For this task, the first Christians provided mothers and fathers in Christ, soul friends, and prayer communities.

Those today who think of the Church as a religious institution conducting Sunday services are simply not paying attention to the real task that Jesus gave us. Most are aware of the Great Commission Jesus gave to the Church in Matthew 28, but they try to fit the great commission into the format of religious services. For them, the task of making disciples has been displaced by the newer calling of building a building and holding Sunday services there. For them, the paradigm of "church" translates into "religion." A Christian is someone who attends services regularly and faithfully. If they do this, they are "good Christians."

At the start, Christians did not have this idea. The first apostles were just trying to do for others what Jesus had done for them. They didn't know any better. They were just being followers of Jesus. Nothing more. Nothing less. True religion, to them, meant "visiting orphans and widows in their distress, and keeping oneself from being polluted by the world" (James 1:27). Love. A pure heart. A good conscience. And all arising from sincere faith. This lifestyle represented a major re-definition of "religion." We get it today by reading the New Testament.

The first apostles changed "religion" into "discipleship." But in the fourth century, Constantine changed discipleship back into religion.

But I believe God wants us all to rediscover the Apostles' original Christian definition, as worked out in the first 700 years of kingdom advance. I have tried to show what this looked like in the Egyptian deserts and in the ancient Celtic Church. Their way of living it out could be instructive for us.

Though Constantine is to be commended for delivering the Church from centuries of Roman persecution, he also delivered the Church *into* a reshaping that would have disastrous consequences during the Middle Ages. However, God always has the last word. Volume Two of this work will concentrate on the more recent "times of refreshing" by which God Himself has intervened to deliver the Church back into the By-My-Spirit patterns described in the Bible: "Not by power, nor by might, but by My Spirit, says the Lord" (Zechariah 4:6). That is the King's decree. It becomes more and more relevant with each passing year.

ENDNOTES

[1] So said Alfred Edersheim, *The Life and Times of Jesus the Messiah, Part II*, p. 397.

[2] The film series, "The Chosen," wonderfully shows Nicodemus, a Pharisee who sat on the Sanhedrin, who *did* see Him. What an amazing portrayal!

[3] I have followed the suggestion of the NIV Study Bible here, placing the Pentecost event inside the Temple. There were "houses" in the temple complex, constructed for the use of groups celebrating feast days. The Temple is the most likely location for the kind of crowds that the story describes.

[4] A fire like this was observable above the building at Azusa during the Azusa Revival, so that, several times, bystanders called the fire department, only to discover that the fire was ephemeral, a sign from God, pointing to His presence in the building. (See Tommy Welchel, *They Told Me Their Stories* [USA: Dare2Dream, 2006], p. 37. The book is full of eye-witness accounts from those who were there.) On the other hand, the fire could have been a manifestation of angels, as Randy Clark has suggested.

[5] It is this extraordinary conviction of sin that will mark virtually every major spiritual awakening in waves of the outpouring of the Holy Spirit in future, as I hope to describe in Volume Two. God is establishing a pattern here that will be amazingly relevant throughout more recent centuries.

[6] This idea about John is borrowed from Alfred Edersheim, *The Temple: Its Ministry and Services as they were at the Time of Christ* (Grand Rapids: Eerdmans, 1982), p. 142.

[7] Another New Testament writer who was intimately acquainted with the temple and who describes the kingdom of God in terms of the temple and its services was the writer of the Book of Hebrews. Tertullian says that this was none other than Barnabas, and the identification fits, for Barnabas was a Levite. See Acts 4:36.

[8] My NIV Study Bible happens to omit the word "presence" (*prosopon*), which is the most important word in the entire chapter. The manifest Presence of God, once isolated to the Holy of Holies, is now being promised to the nations.

[9] Michael Kerrigan, *The Roman Emperors: A Dark History* (New York: Metro, 2008), p. 51.

[10] *Ibid.*, p. 75.

[11] *Ibid.*, p. 76.

[12] *Ibid.*, p. 103.

[13] *Ibid.*, p. 103.

[14] *Ibid.*, p. 107.

[15] See the online version of *Archaeology*, Sept.-Oct., 2015, "Golden House of an Emperor: How archaeologists are saving Nero's fabled pleasure palace," by Federico Gurgone.

[16] Susan Wise Bauer, *The History of the Ancient World* (New York: Norton, 2007), p. 755.

[17] Malachi Martin, *The Decline and Fall of the Roman Church* (New York: Putnam, 1981), pp. 24-26.

[18] Quoted from Susan Wise Bauer, *The History of the Ancient World* (New York: Norton, 2007), pp. 774-775.

[19] Lactantius says that the sign he used was the staurogram, the Latin cross that looks like a "P" on top.

[20] Martin, p. 34.

[21] *Ibid.*, p. 36.

[22] *Ibid.*, p. 38.

[23] Athanasius, *The Life of Anthony* (Mahwah, NJ: Paulist, 1980), p. 38.

[24] *Ibid.*, p. 39.

[25] *Ibid.*, p. 99.

[26] For example, Bruce Ritchie, in his book on Columba, describes a story of St. Antony meeting another hermit named Paul deep in the Egyptian desert, as related by Jerome. "The legend is graphically depicted on the Nigg cross-slab, now preserved in the old Nigg Church in Easter Ross, with another representation on a Pictish cross-slab at St Vigean's. These carvings emphasize Anthony's enduring appeal." (Bruce Ritchie, *The Faith of an Island Soldier* (Ross-shire, GB: Mentor, 2019), p. 33.

[27] *Athanasius*, pp. 42-43.

[28] *Ibid.*, p. 67.

[29] *Ibid.*, p. 72.

[30] *Ibid.*, p. 83.

[31] *Ibid.*, p. 88.

[32] Malachi Martin clarifies: "…There were at least three well-known and authentic lines of legitimate blood descendants from Jesus' own family. One from Joachim and Anna, Jesus' maternal

grandparents. One from Elizabeth, first cousin of Jesus' mother, and Elizabeth's husband Zachary. And one from Cleophas and his wife, who also was a first cousin of Mary." (p. 42).

[33] Martin, p. 44. Douglas Lockhart draws a more positive picture of Sylvester by showing that the *desposyni* had formed themselves into a sect, the Nazoreans, and Sylvester found it necessary to protect the Church from heresy. See www.douglaslockhart.com/the-nazoraean-sect-and-its-independence-from-christianity.

[34] Robert Van de Weyer, *Celtic Fire* (New York: Doubleday, 1990), pp. 7-8.

[35] W. K. Lowther Clarke, trans., *The Lausiac History of Palladius (London, 1918)*, located at evagriusponticus.net).

[36] See monasticmatrix.osu.edu, Ohio State University Dept. of History, "Melania the Younger. "Two biographies of Melania were written shortly after her death: Gerontius, *The Life of Melania the Younger*, and Palladius, *The Lausiac History*.

[37] I have taught this for years and practice it myself. See my teachings, "How Shall We Then Live" at www.TheClearing.us.

[38] Diogenes Allen, *Spiritual Theology* (Cambridge, MA: Cowley, 1997).

[39] *Ibid.*, pp. 77-78.

[40] *Ibid.*, p. 74.

[41] Sulpicius Severus, *The Life of St. Martin*, Nicene and Post-Nicene Fathers of the Christian Church, Volume 11.

[42] Ray Simpson describes the role of Antony's biography on Martin in *Celtic Christianity*, p. 70.

[43] *Sulpicius Severus, Vita, X.*

[44] The Welsh scholar, Norma Lorre Goodrich (*King Arthur* (New York, Harper & Row, 1986) writes: "As the Romans conquered Britain, they recorded the names of the Celtic tribes, just as they had done in Gaul and Belgium. In the border area between what would become the Antonine and Hadrianic Walls, they noted the presence of a population divided into four major tribes, all speaking P-Celtic which today is modern Welsh (as opposed to Irish and Manx, which are Q-Celtic.) These tribes were the Votadini (the Edinburgh area of Lothian), the Selgovae (in the Tweed River valley), the Novantae (in the southwestern area), and the Damnoni (in the valley of the Clyde River, and Glasgow)." The Votadini migrated from this area to the south, to form the nation of Wales. But the ancient home of the Welsh was in the north, in Strathclyde, which extended south into the Lake District in those early days. See pp. 17-24. Bede, on the other hand, says that this area was occupied by "the southern Picts."

[45] *Scotland, Land of Many Revivals, Glory in the Glen,* and *Scotland Ablaze.*

[46] Ray Simpson, *Celtic Christianity*, p. 204.

[47] Ray is the Founder and Guardian of the Aidan and Hilda Society, devoted to rediscovering the lifestyle of the ancient Celts for Christian people today.

[48] *Celtic Christianity*, p. 71.

[49] *Celtic Christianity*, pp. 71-72.

[50] John Cassian, *Conferences* (New York, Paulist, 1985), pp. 40-41.

[51] *Conferences*, p. 55.

[52] *Ibid*, p. 7.

[53] *Ibid*, p. 16.

[54] *Ibid.*, p. 18.

[55] *Ibid.*, p. 21.

[56] *Ibid.*, p. 24.

[57] *Ibid.*, p. 26.

[58] *Ibid.*, p. 28.

[59] *Ibid.*, p. 30.

[60] *Ibid.*, p. 31.

[61] Thomas Cahill, *How the Irish Saved Civilization* (New York: Doubleday, 1995), pp. 123-124.

[62] Ray Simpson, *Celtic Christianity* (Vestal, New York, Anamchara Books, 2017), p. 246.

[63] "The sixteen volume *Lives of the British Saints* by the Reverend Sabine Baring-Gould yields the following: the legends concerning Saint Joseph of Arimathea are wholly worthless (and) they must be passed over." (Goodrich, *King Arthur*, p. 159.)

[64] I am summarizing Haggai, chapters one and two.

[65] The word "Wales" and "Welsh" do not appear until centuries later. The people were known as "Britons." Anglo-Saxons called them "Welsh," meaning "foreign." Eventually, the name stuck.

[66] My *Pocket History of Scotland* says that he was born in Dumbarton (James MacKay, ed., *Pocket History of Scotland* (Bath, England: Lomond), p. 48. Ray Simpson, in *Aidan of Lindisfarne* (Eugene, OR: Stock, 2014), p. 120, suggests Carlisle.

[67] Courtney Davis, for example, in his review of the life of Columba, says that Columba made an important trip to Tours and brought back a Gospel that had lain on the breast of St. Martin; also that Finnian went to Whithorn, not Rome, where he brought

back a copy of St. Martin's Gospel, which became a source of controversy. These stories, at the very least, show the spiritual roots with Martin and Ninian. See *The Book of Celtic Saints* (London: Blandford, 1995), p. 22.

[68] *The Life of Patrick by Muirchù, Celtic Spirituality, The Classics of Western Spirituality* (Mahwah, NJ, Paulist Press, 1999).

[69] Using an expression from Zechariah 12:10, to describe the Holy Spirit as an inspirer of prayer.

[70] *Patrick on the Great Works of God, Celtic Spirituality, The Classics of Western Spirituality* (Mahwah NJ, Paulist Press, 1999), p. 71.

[71] *Ibid.*, p. 73

[72] *Ibid.*, p. 74.

[73] Thomas Cahill, *How the Irish Saved Civilization* (New York: Doubleday, 1995), p. 114.

[74] *Ibid.*, p. 95.

[75] *The Life of Patrick by Muirchù*, p. 96.

[76] Christian missions is full of prophetic stories like this, and I will relate more in my own in Volume Two of this work. See Don Richardson, *Eternity in their Hearts*. Also, his book, *Peace Child*.

[77] *Life of Patrick*, p. 97.

[78] *Ibid.*, pp. 97-98.

[79] The Otis *Transformation* videos are available from Sentinelgroup.org. Darren Wilson's are available from wpfilm.com.

[80] Ibid., p. 108.

[81] Quoted from the Wikipedia article, *"Brigid of Kildare."*

[82] Courtney Davis, *The Book of Celtic Saints* (London: Blandford, 1995), p. 31.

[83] Bruce Ritchie, *Columba: The Faith of an Island Soldier* (Ross-shire, GB: Mentor, 2019), p. 31.

[84] Geoffrey Ashe is an exponent of those who believe that Arthur lived in southern England. Norma Lorre Goodrich argued that Arthur was born in Caerlaverock castle near Whithorn in Strathclyde, in the north.

[85] Geoffrey Ashe, *The Quest for Arthur's Britain* (Chicago: Academy Chicago, 1987), p. 57.

[86] Michael Mitton, *The Soul of Celtic Spirituality in the Lives of its Saints* (Mystic, Connecticut, Twenty-third Publ. 1996), p. 128.

[87] Geoffrey Ashe, *The Quest for Arthur's Britain* (Chicago: Academy Chicago, 1987, 2000), p. 56.

[88] Ray Simpson, who, for many years lived on the Holy Isle of Lindisfarne (where I spent a week with him in 2019), is the ultimate authority about the patterns of the ancient Celtic Church. The best two books that set forth these patterns are: *Celtic Christianity: Deep Roots for a Modern Faith* (Vestal, NY: Anamchara, 2017), and *Soul Friendship: Celtic Insights into Spiritual Mentoring* (London: Hodder & Stoughton, 1999).

[89] Ray Simpson, *Hilda of Whitby: a Spirituality for Now* (Abingdon: Bible Reading Fellowship, 2014), p. 62.

[90] I have taken this whole description from Ray Simpson's writings, and a week spent gaining his teaching on the Isle of Lindisfarne in August, 2019.

[91] The twelve were: Ciaran of Saighir, Ciaran of Clonmacnois, Brendan of Birr, Brendan of Clonfert, Columba of Terryglass,

Columba of Iona, Mobhi of Glasnevin, Ruadhain of Lorrha, Senan of Iniscathay, Ninnidh of Loch Erne, Lasserian mac Nadfraech and Canice of Aghaboe.

[92] The hallway imagery is mine, not Cassian's or Evagrius's. They simply taught the "eight deadly thoughts."

[93] Ray Simpson, *Soul Friendships* (London: Hodder & Stoughton, 1999).

[94] *Ibid.*, p. 11.

[95] *Ibid.*, p. 15.

[96] *Ibid.*, p. 16.

[97] See www.steemit.com for an article about this site, complete with diagrams and photos. Several other articles are available on the internet.

[98] Bruce Ritchie, *Columba: Faith of an Island Soldier* (Ross-shire, Great Britain: Mentor, 2019), p. 362.

[99] *Ibid.*, p. 364.

[100] *Ibid.*, pp. 373-4.

[101] *Ibid.*, p. 53.

[102] The sign of the cross that was used was not the Roman gesture, but the eastern one—just one more quiet indication that the Celts gained their inspiration not from Rome, but from Alexandria and Constantinople.

[103] Adamnan, *The Life of St. Columba* (Edinburgh: Floris, 1992), pp. 29-30.

[104] Available from George Otis, jr. at The Sentinel Group (sentinelgroup.org).

[105] I was horrified to read the article in Wikipedia about this man, which described him as a "Christian." Apparently, the person who wrote this article was unaware that the evil one loves to masquerade behind Christian labels, a form of mockery designed to bring confusion to people like the person who wrote this article.

[106] www.wpfilm.com. The videos of George Otis, jr. are available at www.sentinelgroup.org.

[107] Some say it came from Rome. Also, some say it was Finnian of Movilla, a different Finnian, who possessed the manuscript. But it seems the trend of opinion now is that the two Finnians were one and the same person.

[108] Many historians seem baffled by the attractiveness of these austere monasteries. The solution to this puzzle lies in looking at the old gods, from whom they were being liberated. Thomas Cahill has photographs of the gods, and a couple of chapters about them in *How the Irish Saved Civilization*. The point he makes sums it up: "After the assassination of John F. Kennedy, Daniel Patrick Moynihan was heard to say that to be Irish is to know that in the end the world will break your heart." The point is: If hope costs you everything, it is still worth the price.

[109] From Robert Van de Weyer, *Celtic Fire* (New York, Doubleday, 1990), pp. 57-58.

[110] There were several versions of the Triads, which were a unique method of teaching Welsh history to children by arranging things in groupings of three.

[111] Norma Lorre Goodrich, King Arthur (NY, Harper & Row, 1986), p. 73.

[112] "The Penitential of Cummean," *Celtic Spirituality* (NY: Paulist, 1999), p. 230.

[113] Gregory the Great, *The Life of St. Benedict*, Terrence G. Kardong, tr. (Collegeville, MN, Liturgical Press, 2009).

[114] *Ibid.*, pp. 62-63.

[115] Bede, *Ecclesiastical History of the English People* (London, Penguin, 1955, 1990), p. 104. Book Two launches into a panegyric in praise of Gregory the Great and his man Augustine.

[116] *Ibid.*, p. 105.

[117] *Ibid.*, p. 106.

[118] Ray Simpson, *Aidan of Lindisfarne* (Eugene, Oregon: Resource Publ., 2014), p. 80.

[119] *Aidan*, pp. 81, 201. The story was told by Oswald to Failbe, Abbot of Iona, who told it to Adamnan. Oswald named the site of victory "Heaven's Field." It became a place of frequent healing of sicknesses.

[120] *Aidan*, p. 85. Bede, p. 151. This is Ray Simpson's fictionalized account of Aidan's speech, described more briefly by Bede and Adamnan. Aidan will exemplify the words of Paul, "I became all things to all men, that I might win some to Christ." His was a contextualized Gospel, so different from what Augustine and Paulinus brought from Rome.

[121] Ritchie, p. 357.

[122] *Ibid.*, p. 152.

[123] Ray Simpson, *Aidan of Lindisfarne*, pp. 126-127.

[124] Courtney Davis, *The Book of Celtic Saints* (London: Blandford, 1995), p. 51.

[125] *Aidan*, p. 131. Let me share a similar experience of Kingdom authority I know of today: Norma Blacksmith, a Lakota Christian woman, an acquaintance of mine, recently spoke with authority to a prairie fire that was threatening the village of Oglalla in South Dakota recently, and she turned back the fire with the words: "Thus far and no farther." The fire stopped just where she commanded. Norma is full of stories of authoritative Kingdom prayer on the Pine Ridge reservation in South Dakota. These stories, confirmed by others on Pine Ridge, were reported at a George Otis conference in Kansas City in May, 2019. Many other stories have been reported in George Otis's *Sentinel Group* newsletters.

[126] *Aiden, p.* 133.

[127] *Ibid.*, p. 149.

[128] This story is from Bede, p. 166 and Simpson, *Aidan,* p. 149.

[129] *Aidan*, pp. 151-152.

[130] Of Aidan, he writes: "I greatly admire and love all these things about Aidan, because I have no doubt that they are pleasing to God; but I cannot approve or commend his failure to observe Easter at the proper time...." (Bede, p. 170.)

[131] East Anglia had come to Christ through the conversion of King Earpwald in 627. But, once again, when the king was killed, the whole nation had fallen away from Christ, right back into paganism. It makes you wonder about the wisdom of converting nations by converting kings.

[132] Agilbert, however, became a supporter of Rome, despite his training in Ireland.

[133] Bede, pp. 177-178.

[134] The NIV Study Bible notes clarify Paul's true meaning: "*Submit to one another.* Basic to the following paragraphs. Paul will show how, in each relationship, each partner can have a conciliatory attitude that will help that relationship. The grammar indicates that this mutual submission is associated with the filling of the Spirit in v. 18. The command 'be filled' (v. 18) is followed by a series of participles in the Greek: speaking (v. 19), singing (v. 19), making music (v. 19), giving thanks (v. 20) and submitting (v. 21)."

[135] It is said that this story is where J.R.R. Tolkien got his idea for the "fellowship of the ring."

[136] The story, and its historical evidence, are found in *Aidan of Lindisfarne*, pp. 116-119, 210-211.

[137] In her day, she was quite famous; her life was not written up until the 13th century.

[138] Simpson, *Hilda of Whitby*, p. 51.

[139] Bede tells us very little about Hilda. Ray Simpson comments: "Bede was not interested in women." (*Hilda*, p.52.)

[140] The hymn, like the story, is from *Ecclesiastical History*, pp. 248-249.

[141] *Aidan of Lindisfarne*, p. 214.

[142] Wilfrid's career is presented in the most favorable possible light by Bede. However, it is not hard to read between the lines as he describes the conflicts between these two very strong-willed men. (Bede, pp. 302-303.)

[143] Unpublished paper, "The Passover Controversy in the East and West," Cambridge University, 2004.

[144] See Rabbi David Rudolph's review of the history and importance of this issue, in his article, "The Science of Worship:

Astronomy, Intercalation, and the Church's Dependence on the Jewish People," at www.rabbidavid.net. Rabbi David reviews the blatant anti-Semitism that was behind the insistence on rejecting Jewish tradition. He quotes in its entirety the letter that Polycrates wrote to Victor on this controversy.

[145] Ray Simpson, *Aidan of Lindisfarne*, p. 193.

[146] The Greek actually says, "whatever you bind on earth *will have been bound* in heaven," meaning that God will cause us to align our prayers with His kingly authority and power, as we bind demonic power. It does not mean that we get to pray whatever we want, and God must grant it because we are praying in Jesus' Name.

[147] *Hilda of Whitby*, p. 79.

[148] Bede, pp. 188-189.

[149] Bede, p. 191-2.

[150] Ritchie, *Columba*, pp. 67-68.

[151] The word, *arrabon* from Ephesians 1:14 is translated as "earnest" or "down-payment," indicating a beginning of an inheritance in kind, that will be given in full at a later date. Earnest money promising complete fulfillment when King Jesus returns "to restore all things."

[152] Brad Long and I gave some historical perspective on the Baptism of the Holy Spirit in our book, *Receiving the Power* (Grand Rapids: Chosen, 1996).

[153] "Power tends to corrupt; absolute power corrupts absolutely."

[154] Frank Bartleman, *Azusa Street* (New Kensington, PA, Whitaker House, 1982), p. 13.

[155] Brad Long and I developed the teachings of "The Dunamis Project," which help people open up to these realities. The Dunamis Project is a series of five-day conferences put on by Presbyterian-Reformed Ministries International around the world (www.PRMI. org). PRMI is represented in various nations by teams of leaders called Dunamis Fellowships.

CPSIA information can be obtained
at www.ICGtesting.com
Printed in the USA
BVHW040822250921
617379BV00004B/6